CW00641492

PREVIOUS ENGAGEMENTS

The author, 1945

PREVIOUS ENGAGEMENTS

Bruce Shand

MICHAEL RUSSELL

For Tom and Ben

First published in Great Britain 1990
by Michael Russell (Publishing) Ltd
The Chantry, Wilton, Salisbury, Wiltshire
Typeset by Dave Sullivan Typesetting
Oakdale, Poole, Dorset
Printed and bound in Great Britain
by Biddles Ltd, Guildford and King's Lynn

ISBN 0 85955 169 5

Contents

Introduction	7
Approach	9
Encounter	40
Intermission	60
Re-Encounter	82
Suspension	140
Maps	168
Index	173

Introduction

In the late summer of 1941, just before sailing for the Middle East, I went to call on an old friend of my grandmother, living in Bath. He had been a distinguished Gunner general and he wanted to ask me about the operations in May 1940. I told him what I could and he then started talking of his past service – not, happily for me, about the First World War (I was dreading endless reminiscences of creeping barrages), but of his life as a young man in the South African War, living in the open, in possession of perfect health, and happy in the excitements and comradeship of the campaign. He was a good raconteur and I was a very willing listener, but with the obtuseness of youth – I was twenty-four at the time – I felt that this was a tenuous link with remote history.

In fact the Boer War had ended less than forty years before. In the intervening time had taken place what the more blimpish characters described as the 'Kaiser's Show'. Now one suddenly realises that 'Hitler's Show' started half a century ago and it will not be long before there will be few or no survivors left to tell their tales. So with diffidence I have ventured to put together my modest personal records, which are those of a junior regular regimental officer, in the hope that they may be of minor interest.

The shape of the narrative resembles that monstrous comestible, a club sandwich. There are two strata of filling, and three of bread. The filling is made up of two accounts that I wrote while a prisoner in the latter half of the war. I managed to send these home through either the Swiss or Swedish Red Cross, but they were impounded by the Historical Section of the War Office and I was unable to obtain possession of them until 1970. They comprise details of my activities in France and Belgium in 1940, and in North Africa in 1941-42. The first account was put together three years after the events it describes, the second within a matter of months. When writing them I was conscious that they would have to pass through both German and British censorship and possibly that imposed reticence makes them, in retrospect, somewhat anaemic. They are printed as written some forty-five years ago with only minor alterations of syntax and spelling and a few excisions to avoid repetition.

The three pieces of bread relate to the so-called 'Phoney War', to England in 1940-41 and to my period of incarceration. The middle one benefits from a diary which I kept at that time, the two outer pieces depend entirely on treacherous memory and a few letters home.

Many have given me help, encouragement and occasionally the spur. To all of them I extend my grateful thanks.

Approach

It may be recalled that Mr Neville Chamberlain, returning from one of his discussions with Adolf Hitler in the late summer of 1938, chose to quote from *King Henry IV Part One* that 'out of this nettle, danger, we pluck this flower, safety'.

By 3 September of the following year it was apparent that his gardening expertise had been as successful as his early sisal-growing activities in the Bahamas, and even thoughtless and hedonistic young men such as myself realised, some time before this date, that war would shortly be upon us, though in what precise shape was anyone's guess. Maybe it was a little premature to say 'Now thrive the armourers', but the amateur strategists were already in great speculating voice.

On that Sunday morning as we listened on the radio to the weary voice of the Prime Minister, mobilisation was already in full flood in Warburg Barracks, Aldershot, the Victorian pile where the 12th Lancers were then housed. Reservists appeared in large numbers, seemingly ancient officers arrived in outdated uniforms, our chargers were whisked away to help mount a horsed division, and the quartermaster (a beloved and enormously capable man called Bill Mabbott) and his staff went into top gear to feed, clothe and generally succour the enlarged regiment. There was certainly an atmosphere of excitement, if not of euphoria, and a sense of relief that at last something was happening. Inevitably there were those who were taking the situation extremely seriously and others, among whom I must number myself, who possibly assumed a more relaxed view or, as we expressed it at the time, a more philosophical one; and indeed my great friend Neil Speke and I had already been in trouble for venturing to go for a ride on the second or third day of mobilisation. When reprimanded; we pointed out that the system was so efficient that there was little for us to do for the moment – a statement which was accepted with some suspicion and scepticism.

At this dramatic date I had been in the Army for nearly three years, having joined from Sandhurst in early 1937. There was no glut of military tradition in my rather strange family. Two of my paternal grandfather's uncles had held commissions in the mid-nineteenth century, one in the 69th Foot, subsequently selling out while in India and disappearing to Australia, and the other in the East India Company's service (HEICS). He died young as, according to his nephew, he had been imprudently drinking too much before going out into the hot sun ('I'm afraid he was a bit of a blackguard also, my dear boy').

My stepfather, although not a regular soldier, had fought with gallantry in the 1914 war and had retained a taste for the Army, with a considerable knowledge of its uniforms, history and traditions. Perhaps some of this rubbed off on me during a rather *mouvementé* childhood, and I have certainly remained fascinated by its pomp and circumstance, if not with some of its less romantic administrative aspects. I do not think I harboured many martial ambitions and neither the baton of a field-marshal nor even the pace stick of a sergeant-major ever entered my subconscious, to give Freudian significance to my dreams.

My Shand grandmother, to whom I was very attached, had a fair amount of say in my upbringing. She had close affiliations with the medical profession and obviously would have liked to have been a doctor herself – her father, brother and nephew were all physicians in Bath, the former achieving some eminence. There were also strong mercantile links with Liverpool, where her grandfather, nicknamed 'Halfpenny Hope', had been an obtrusively pious and parsimonious citizen. To me he sounded excessively dreary, but I held my peace as his last remaining child, my Great-Great-Aunt Fetty (Miss Septima Hope, the seventh daughter of thirteen siblings), who lived to be nearly a hundred, was thought to look favourably upon me. As far as my grandmother was concerned, medicine or banking would be the suitable professions for me.

With these aspirations in mind, she was anxious that I should not go to Eton where both her husband and son (with neither of whom, sadly, had she enjoyed particularly harmonious relationships) were set on the road to modest intellectual prowess. Rather illogically, and I think unfairly, she attributed the plethora of wives, four in all, that my father collected to the influence of that seat of learning.

Accordingly, I was despatched to Rugby, a school I cordially disliked and where I spent some four not necessarily unhappy but infinitely drab years. My clerical housemaster, a mathematical Mr Quiverful, was a nice enough man. He had been a military acquaintance of my stepfather in the war before taking the cloth, but was beset with domestic distractions in the shape of his innumerable children. He retained his interest in military matters, still going out enthusiastically with the OTC, and I think endeavoured to foster some similar interest in me, to the further detriment of the medical and banking hopes of my grandmother, which were already getting scant enough encouragement. Eventually, after passing the requisite exams (the School Certificate in those days), I left Rugby having learnt very little and having made practically no friends – on the whole a pretty unsatisfactory boy, rather indolent, self-conscious and invertebrate. I had, however, become an omnivorous reader and developed a love of horses and riding, with the result that there was a tacit family agreement that it would be better for me to go into the Army for a few years rather than walk the hospitals or get to grips with the mysteries of the counting house. What was to happen thereafter was anyone's guess.

I was sent briefly to France to try and learn the language

but this visit was cut short owing to my grandfather's death. So I went to a crammer in St George's Square, Pimlico, presided over by a Mr McNalty. Thanks to its admirable instructors, I passed quite well into Sandhurst, despite having become, rather like my great-great-uncle, 'imprudently' drunk on the second night of the exams.

Sandhurst in 1935 was quite tough and probably much the same as it had been half a century or more before. The first term involved immense amounts of foot drill, a great deal of cleaning of equipment and a few academic periods of study which were chiefly welcomed for the chance of being able to sit down. I managed to survive. In the second term riding was part of the curriculum, as were gymnastics. The latter were sheer hell – I have always been hopeless at any game or form of athletics and one had to be a certain shape to carry out the contortions required for the obligatory tests. For those not of the standard size, there were spells of extra physical tuition at the hands of somewhat sadistic instructors. Thankfully the riding school was a much easier and happier proposition. In the last of the three terms time was allotted to what was called 'car maintenance', presumably in view of the impending mechanisation of the Army.

I was in No. 1 Company in the new building, under the command of an agreeable and quiet major in the Welch Regiment called Cripps. I believe in the latter part of the war he became Military Governor of Naples and in some way saved the San Carlo Opera House from demolition, thereby rightly becoming an Italian hero and doubtless, and suitably, a '*Commendatore*'. He did not worry us unduly. Apart from our sergeant-major, Dusty Smith, a warrant officer in the Coldstream Guards with an interesting and almost poetic vocabulary ('I've had men through my hands from the bogs of Ireland, the moors of Scotland and the claypits of Staffordshire, but none so idle as you gentlemen'), the figure that loomed most in our lives was a captain in the Royal Fusiliers, one Shaggy Ransome.

Resembling a more hirsute Robert Louis Stevenson, he was a mine of military lore and advice. The three vital precepts on which to base the life of a officer were: 1 The key to military discipline is close order drill; 2 If the officers' mess drinks then the sergeants' mess drinks, so do the corporals, and in fact the whole regiment drinks; 3 Leave is a privilege and never a right. To these was added a very strong warning against venturing into Reading in search of carnal pleasure. None of us had pinpointed that particular town as a centre for Paphian delights, and I suspect all Shaggy's guidelines were of doubtful practical value to us. However, they did him no harm at all: he soared ahead in the military hierarchy and, I think, ended the war as a major-general.

I achieved no distinction at Sandhurst apart from riding in 'The Saddle' and against Woolwich, and passed out lower than I passed in; but I made a lot of friends and remain more than grateful to that establishment for putting some life and backbone into a rather amorphous and disorganised adolescent.

My name had been entered for a certain well-known cavalry regiment, should I eventually achieve a commission. This was the way matters were managed in those days and I had been provisionally accepted by its colonel, thanks to the assistance of a mutual acquaintance. Two fellow cadets, both friends of mine, were in line for the same regiment, one of whose officers happened to be on the Sandhurst staff. For reasons only partially understandable, he took a dislike to all three of us. He advised that we should not be accepted.

Since we were all nearing the end of our last term, there was inevitably some panic and confusion before we could be re-located. Kim Muir, charming, dashing and far too rich, went to the 10th Hussars to be killed in France in 1940. He was a great steeplechaser and there is a race in his memory at Cheltenham. Tim Llewellen-Palmer, the youngest of four splendid brothers, two of whom were also to be killed, joined the 7th Hussars, where he had a very distinguished and highly individual career before too early a death. And I was sent for by the Commandant, Bertie Fisher, and told that Colonel McCreery of the 12th Lancers was coming over to Sandhurst shortly to interview me.

Dick McCreery, whom I came to venerate, was initially slightly frightening and austere, though probably as shy as I was; he also had quite a considerable temper, as I was deservedly to find out later on. He was at pains, however, to be friendly and his somewhat severe features could relax into the most charming and unexpected smile. We sat in a little room adjoining the adjutant's office and I remember thinking he was rather old. In fact he was not yet thirty-nine and had obtained command at what was then a very early age. He seemed to know something about me and at the end of our conversation, which included a question from him on the delicate subject of 'means', it was settled that I should join the regiment at Tidworth early in the new year (1937), subject to my passing out adequately. We shook hands and I watched him walk to his car with that very idiosyncratic gait (the result of a severe First War wound) which would become so familiar to thousands of soldiers in Italy by the end of the war.

A few months later, not without trepidation, I took myself to Tidworth, preceded by a mountain of luggage that included a sword bearing the cipher of the recently abdicated King Edward VIII (who was also Colonel of the 12th Lancers). I had a chestnut horse called The Bashaw, given me the previous summer, which I had been hunting intermittently with the Cottesmore. One of my Sandhurst friends, George Murray-Smith, and his mother Olive had a house for that winter near Oakham. Thanks to their kindness I made my first visit to the 'Grass Countries', gaining a taste for the excitement of pre-war foxhunting in Leicestershire.

The regiment had only recently returned again from Egypt; it had completed a six-year term abroad there only to be recalled when Mussolini started making bellicose noises in the Mediterranean. There were very few people about as most were on leave and in any case the establishment of officers was then very small (no subaltern had joined in four years). It seemed uncertain as to what should be done with me. My immediate superiors were Tony Warre and Tim Morris. Fortunately I had met them both previously and they could not have been more friendly and helpful. Tony, a star of the Beaufort Hunt and enjoying a notable success everywhere on account of his charm and good looks, is happily still with us, appearing little older after half a century. Tim, more cosmopolitan (he had a French-Swiss mother), was also a dashing character, a thin black moustache giving emphasis to his Beau Sabreur outlook. Sadly he died, prematurely, some few years ago. Thanks to these two, I was steered into the right channels and took quick notice of their views on our brother officers.

Everyone was very welcoming and the atmosphere was relaxed and quite unlike anything Shaggy Ransome had so ghoulishly described to us when discussing our 'first appointments'. I was assigned to the squadron of Ian Smith (called 'British' Smith by the troops), an officer of considerable eccentricity and lack of humour, but a master of administrative detail. I received general sympathy at being placed with him and errors and blunders that I subsequently made were partially excused because of my unlucky circumstances. Later on, Bill Carr, a marvellous horseman, with an Italian wife of great character, took me into his tutelage, which was entirely beneficent.

'British' did not initially have much to say in my life. I was taken under the wing of Frank Arkwright, the adjutant, as nice a man as ever lived and a quietly efficient soldier. I was profoundly indebted to him as he not only pulled me out of various scrapes, without necessarily informing the colonel, but also judiciously handed me over to certain senior NCOs who took my education in hand and tactfully but firmly directed my floundering steps. They were very competent nannies with a decidedly un-nannylike capacity for beer. With the hindsight of half a century I salute their memory and especially Bill Mabbott, already mentioned. He was then Mr Mabbott, the regimental sergeant-major, but subsequently became a wonderfully dependable quartermaster. A model of smartness and loyalty allied to almost complete selflessness, he was to be a godsend to the regiment and its commanding officers. The then quartermaster, Uncle Lawrence, was living in the mess and very helpful he was as well. A charming and modest person, deeply versed in regimental history, he had won a DCM on the retreat from Mons. He was a fount of information – not least about the characters and eccentricities of past and present officers, including the remarkable succession of commanding officers we had had during the past fifteen years or so.

In the early Twenties the 12th Lancers, like most regiments at some period in their existence, struck a bad patch. This had been rectified when 'Bloody' Mike Blakiston-Houston was brought in from the 11th Hussars, making Dick McCreery his adjutant and sacking half a dozen over-lighthearted officers. Mike Blakiston-Houston was widely renowned both for his language, said to rival that of the Duke of Cambridge, and for his energy. (To meet in later life, he was the epitome of courtesy and friendliness but I observed that those who had served with him were apt to lose colour and develop nervous twitches in his presence.) However, he achieved impressive results which were maintained by his four successors.

When mechanisation had taken place in 1928 and the horses had been replaced by armoured cars, the transition had been commendably smooth thanks to capability all round and imagination at the top. By the time I joined, a long spell abroad had created a highly efficient entity, only marred by the totally inadequate equipment provided by an under-funded War Office at the mercy of the Government.

During its time in Egypt the regiment had carried out

desert reconnaissances to such remote places as the Siwa and Farafra oases in the Libyan Desert, with expeditions, too, as far south as Wadi Halfa. These had proved of enormous value in a variety of ways, not least in the competence and confidence that came from all ranks having to think for themselves. Indeed they even affected the activities of such a neophyte as myself who not infrequently (and often at great personal inconvenience) was told to take a troop of three armoured cars and two despatch riders, perhaps fourteen men in all, to some remote part of the kingdom for a couple of days and keep in touch on the wireless. It was good experience. Disasters occurred, not always reported back and loyally forgotten by those soldiers who had to suffer for my shortcomings, but probably I learnt more than I realised on these outings, even though I was chiefly occupied in fulminating against the military fate which had prevented me from going to some glamorous entertainment in London.

At that time our principal vehicles were old Lanchester armoured cars that had seen plenty of service, but we were able to fulfil mobile roles and, especially in the three summers before the war, carried out a good deal of training in the field. Looking back, I suspect that standards of driving, gunnery and map-reading were very high; added to which there was, for those days, a very sophisticated familiarity with the use of radio communication, then still something of a novelty and even an object of suspicion in the British Army. We had the benefit of an attached troop of the Royal Corps of Signals under a brilliant officer called George Balmain, and he and his men did much to perfect the different levels of inter-squadron and troop radio links, both in long and short range. To give an indication of the former, as early as 1932 Christmas greetings had been exchanged over the air from Cairo with the 11th Hussars in England. They had been mechanised at the same time as ourselves and both regiments, having armoured car roles, were closely connected in matters of training and personnel. The other cavalry regiments at Tidworth, where we spent two years, were trying to understand tanks and were probably envious of us for having all our conversion troubles long behind us and for being more mobile.

The brigadier, Cecil Heydeman (disliked, I think, by Dick McCreery), who had formerly commanded the Bays, was a somewhat picaresque character; Jewish, intelligent, idle and cultivated, he was to have a rather mixed future. By the beginning of the war he had become a major-general, only a little junior in the Army List to B.L. Montgomery. By 1945 he was still a major-general, in charge of some military district in Italy where it seemed he had got into fearful trouble for trying to murder a lady who was either his current wife or mistress.

On one occasion he invited Tony Warre and myself to dine with him after a cocktail party. Hoping that the colonel was unaware of our destination, we followed him to his official house – he was then temporarily unmarried – which was full of French eighteenth-century furniture, though whether genuine or not I cannot say. Dinner was bibulous to say the least of it and we were treated to a spate of reminiscence, much of it lubricious. But I chiefly recall his saying that he had been fortunate enough to have witnessed three quite remarkable events in his life, the first of which had been when Teddy Brooks had jumped the level-crossing gates at Long Clawson – presumably just in front of the Flying Scotsman. (Teddy Brooks had been a celebrated horseman before the First World War and Long Clawson lies in the Belvoir country.)

We were suitably impressed and awaited the second episode. This concerned the first use of tanks at the Battle of Cambrai when dramatic tactical surprise had been achieved and 'changed history', so he said.

He was a good raconteur and both these occurrences had been described in considerable detail, assisted by an equally considerable amount of brandy. A pause ensued while we awaited the third and final revelation. The silence became somewhat prolonged and the narrator possibly a little somnolent and eventually we ventured to remind him that he had something more to tell us. 'Brigadier, what was the third remarkable event?' 'I'm damned if I can remember.'

Despite nearly a decade of mechanisation the horse still played a very prominent part in our lives. Officers still had two government chargers each, which were seldom required to do anything other than hunt, or play polo if they were the right size. This perquisite had been granted as a sop at the time of mechanisation in 1928. These horses received a full ration of forage throughout the year and in addition one had a military groom or second servant (the first servant looked after one's uniform and personal comfort). The regiment had a great polo reputation and contained some notable players, not least Dick McCreery himself who excelled in all equine activities and many others as well. In the four years up to the war it had always been in the final of the Inter-Regimental Cup, winning it in 1936. The game was taken very seriously, with portentous tactical conferences which verged on the comic to those who were not in the first flight – which certainly included me, although I was able to be of modest help in schooling people's ponies. Had I played the game in England I should probably have ended up in the bankruptcy court. I already had too many hunters and despite the generous allowance from my grandmother, boosted by a legacy from Aunt Fetty, managed to outrun the constable handsomely.

Military pay in those days was practically non-existent. It just covered one's mess bills with luck, and as I was inclined to both extravagance and folly and aspired to a life compounded by images of Charles O'Malley and Count d'Orsay, sooner or later something drastic would have occurred. In all likelihood I think I would have had to consider being seconded to one of those overseas forces (British officers and native troops) which then helped to keep the Empire together. Probably there were some fifteen or twenty of these organisations at that time, offering higher pay and rank and the opportunity of active service. A redoubtable member of the regiment, 'Dozy' Willis, had just returned from a stint with the Trans-Jordan Frontier Force (where he had won an MC) and I daresay I might have gravitated there in other circumstances, as it sounded exciting and had the advantage of still being partly horsed. Certainly another three years in England before the regiment went abroad again would have proved fatal for my economic condition. As it was, the seismic upheaval of 1939 altered everything for everybody and the scope for extravagance was for the time being curtailed.

During the year or two leading up to this we had been taking delivery of the Morris armoured car. This was stigmatised as being under-engined, under-armed and under-armoured, but the description was only partially true. The armament comprised a Bren gun and a Boys anti-tank rifle, not exactly 'heavy' weapons, and the metal plating was pretty thin. There was no top cover other than a piece of canvas, meant to keep out the rain, but with good maintenance, good drivers and a bit of tinkering it could show a fair turn of speed.

We had also acquired a new colonel, Herbert Lumsden. When I joined, I think he was teaching at the Staff College and he was only seen when he returned to ride in, and usually win, our regimental races. He was an outstanding amateur steeplechase jockey and at that time had the riding of Lord Stalbridge's horses; but for the war he would probably have been aboard the winner of the 1940 Grand National, Bogskar. Originally a Horse Gunner, he had a very sharp mind, a very smart appearance and possibly a greater tolerance of human error than his predecessor (who may well have concealed it). Ambitious, but blessed with humour and humanity, he was to make a considerable reputation for himself and his regiment.

Mobilisation brought us up to war strength but the force we could deploy was very meagre. There were three squadrons, each consisting of three troops of three armoured cars, with three more cars in each squadron headquarters and three at regimental headquarters, in all thirty-nine armoured cars. In addition each troop had a couple of motor-cyclist despatch riders. Lorries and other vehicles were by no means of a universal pattern as many of them were impressed from civilian sources pending the arrival of more uniform types of transport. As may be imagined, this led to many complications over spare parts and so on.

In the shake-up I had a troop in 'A' Squadron commanded by Andrew Horsbrugh-Porter, one of the stars of the regimental polo team, a Wykehamist, very brave but with something of 'a temperament', no doubt springing from a fair measure of Irish and, I believe, Spanish ancestry. We had always got on well and I was glad to be placed with him as he always evinced great cavalry dash and had been something of an ally of mine in my difficulties with 'British' Smith.

Rodney Palmer was our second in command, a dear fellow, a member of that eminent Berkshire philanthropic biscuit family and later on a most successful breeder of foxhounds (and indeed of other animals). He was most thorough in everything that he undertook. At Tidworth he hunted the local hounds, the Tedworth, and Tony Warre and I assisted him, perhaps rather lightheartedly, on hound exercise and cub hunting, as amateur whippers-in. I recall on one occasion he was very upset that I had failed to count the amount of hounds which had 'emptied' themselves. Thereafter I reported, not always accurately, any signs of canine constipation.

Immediately after the outbreak of war there was a panic about air raids and nearly all the garrison of Aldershot was moved to outlying Hampshire villages, a complex administrative operation, coming as it did directly after mobilisation. I was fortunate enough to be put in charge of what was called

'Passive Air Defence' in our barracks, so remained comfortably there with a few men and a vintage fire engine, very uncertain in its emission of water, while my brother officers roughed it among the grass widows of the surrounding countryside.

During these early days of September we were expecting any day to leave England with other troops from Aldershot who were already on their way to France, but suddenly were told that there was no further use for armoured cars and that they were to be handed in. Instead we were to start retraining for Cruiser tanks. This ludicrous War Office order was symptomatic of the confusion that then prevailed. To require that troops who had been trained for some eleven years in a specific role should be asked to forget it and prepare to learn about non-existent tanks was entering into the area of military cloud-cuckoo-land. Luckily Herbert Lumsden kept a cool head, as ever, realising that Sir John Dill, Commander of the 1st Corps, was anxious to have us. By early October, the War Office having relented, we were ready to embark for France.

By a curious coincidence the regiment left the same barracks in Aldershot on the identical date, 15 October, as it had exactly forty years before, to go to the South African War. Tim Bailey, one of our young officers, had invited his father Percy (himself a distinguished 12th Lancer) to dine a night or two before we went. He told us that on the eve of departure in 1899 he had been at some splendid party in London and had missed the last train to Aldershot. However he had gone to the best hansom-cab stand, which was apparently in Park Lane, and found a driver with a good horse to take him back to Aldershot for a fiver, provided the horse could be put up the next day. There had been no problem and he had bowled into the barracks in a tailcoat as the dawn was coming up, and first and second servants had horses and baggage and uniform ready for the march out an hour or two later.

I only wished, in my nostalgic way, that it was still like

that as the advance party with the bulk of the vehicles travelled to Southampton. Having had these removed to be loaded into ships, we were then incarcerated in some hotel with various other officers for a day or two of what I remember as continuous insobriety. Eventually the advance party boarded a transport and after a night at sea disembarked, bleary-eyed, to join the rest of the regiment on the quayside at Cherbourg.

The younger men naïvely imagined that they would soon be reunited with their armoured cars and lorries but these, apparently not lost at sea, had disappeared elsewhere, not to be seen again for several days. In the meantime we were required to march, as no other means of transport was available, to the Château de Martinvaast some miles south of Cherbourg.

Loaded with overcoats and a fair amount of kit we set forth, not in the blithest of spirits, under a surprisingly hot October sun. We were less than delighted by the sight of a long line of French lorries standing empty while their drivers took a midday snooze in a side street, but morale rose at the prospect of the somewhat sedentary orderly room staff sweltering under heavy loads and subjected to unaccustomed exercise.

Martinvaast, of which I still have a photograph, is or was a hefty fifteenth-century castle, the home of the Pourtalès family, distinguished both as diplomats and as pillars of French racing. I seem to remember that there was a stud there and that the Comte de Pourtalès and Andrew Horsbrugh-Porter engaged in prolonged discussion of blood lines and that the whole family was immensely hospitable with delightful old-fashioned manners. The troops were all bedded down in the various outbuildings and the officers distributed throughout the château. About a dozen of us slept in the State Bedroom and for some reason it was thought appropriate that I should occupy the Great Bed, on which my humble sleeping bag had been laid out. We passed a rather disturbed night, not made easier by Andrew and Dozy Willis having a blazing row in an adjoining dressing-room.

The following day we were transported to some local station and there the officers were enclosed hermetically in carriages which must have been in use during the Second Empire. The soldiers were packed into ancient wagons labelled 'Hommes quarantes, chevaux huits' and we settled down in our plush-lined compartments without corridors, let alone loos. We steamed gently through France for a day and a half, being fed by occasional baskets of food poked through the window. Little information could be obtained of our destination and the relief of nature was a chancy business as it was never certain for how long the train would stop; sometimes it was for several hours, sometimes for two minutes.

Eventually, stations began to bear names familiar from the First World War and it was apparent that we were approaching the Pas de Calais. At Arras we finally halted, expecting to find our own transport, but again we were lifted by strange lorries and the evening found the regiment in various villages to the south west. In the end we were not to go to 1st Corps but were to be GHQ troops, billeted near Lord Gort and his headquarters. There were inevitably hiccups over the initial arrangements but 'A' Squadron ended up in the village of Fonquevillers, which was to be our home for the next six months. Like most of its neighbours, it had been completely flattened in the First War and the surrounding country was dreary, without features or even many mature trees. Military cemeteries were dotted about in profusion and although all the old trenches had disappeared, the atmosphere of the previous war seemed very close; in fact all the senior officers with the BEF were survivors from it, many of them deeply imbued with the static tactics which had characterised its bloody operations.

Our vehicles eventually arrived and we endeavoured to sort ourselves out, with training starting again as we settled down to wait. But for what? France was still a great military nation standing behind her Maginot Line and the BEF, only mustering two army corps, was a sort of poor relation. The only contact with the Germans at this time was in the area of the Saar where 'patrol activity' took place. It was a curious period and every effort had to be made to counteract boredom. It was also a period that did not suit our volatile squadron leader.

It seemed to be envisaged that at some moment there would be an advance into the Low Countries, particularly once Belgium had overcome her condition of nervous neutrality. If this occurred we would be in contact, as the advanced reconnaissance element of the BEF, with certain French troops, and therefore our first priority was to establish some sort of cooperation. Herbert Lumsden, rightly, put much emphasis on this task and it was to pay off well.

The French troops with whom we were to work were of a very high quality, I would imagine regulars and regular reservists. They belonged to the very well equipped Divisions Légères Mecanisées (DLM) of which there were then only three in the French Army. Their armoured cars were Panhards with substantial armour plating, mounting a heavy machine gun and a most effective anti-tank gun. They were probably slower than our flimsy Morrises, but they could travel backwards when required, with the wireless operator driving, so that they did not have the turmoil of turning round in an emergency. The tanks of these divisions were Hotchkiss 35 and Somua 39 and very impressive they were.

In order to facilitate relations with these formations and with the French in general, we had an 'agent de liaison' with regimental headquarters and with each squadron. I think Herbert must have exerted influence somewhere appropriate, as they were all men of intelligence and adaptability, as well as being completely bilingual. For some reason, probably French military parsimony, they were not given commissioned rank but they all lived in our messes, whose comforts they greatly enhanced. Initially in 'A' Squadron we had a youngish man with an English name, François Fenwick, but early in the new year he was replaced by Henry de la Falaise, who not only contributed to our wellbeing and was a delightful companion but was of inestimable courage during the coming campaign. (In 1943 he was to publish in the USA a book entitled, rather dramatically, *Through Hell to Dunkirk*. He had kept a diary during May 1940, and on the whole it gave a very fair description of the activities of our squadron, to whose memory it was dedicated.)

Of an ancient and, I think, impecunious family, he had fought with gallantry in the First World War, receiving not only the Croix de Guerre but also the coveted Médaille Militaire, and was badly wounded. Extremely smart and well-dressed at all times, he had a strong resemblance to a film star of those days called Adolf Menjou, though I believe the latter had no French blood. Henry's knowledge of the celluloid world and of Hollywood in particular was encyclopedic as he had gone to make his fortune there very soon after the war, employed at one time by Joseph Kennedy, subsequently American Ambassador in England, of whose early commercial activities he painted the most lurid and terrifying picture. His fortune he had not made, though he had managed to marry in succession Gloria Swanson and Constance Bennett. By 1940 he had long been rid of the former and was now disenchanted with the latter and was hoping to wed a charming and very rich South American, Emmita Rodriguez. Constance Bennett was being difficult about the divorce but just before the Blitzkrieg started Henry received incontrovertible evidence of her adultery. His only fear, and nothing else seemed to alarm him during the next three weeks, was that he might lose these vital papers. Happily they reached England with him. It was a real pleasure to have him with us: good-tempered and good-mannered, amusing and with time for everyone and with a generosity of spirit not always apparent in his compatriots, the 'Marquee', as the troops called him, was an enormous asset, especially as Andrew had great respect for him and consequently acted in a more restrained manner than hitherto. Henry was highly conscientious in smoothing over matters with the inhabitants of Fonquevillers when difficulties arose over billets, drunken troops and so on.

The district seemed bereft of doctors – presumably all the French ones had been mobilised – so medical officers serving with the BEF found themselves in constant demand among the civilian population. As a result of this and the fact that Henry was away in Paris with the beloved Emmita, I became involuntarily involved with unexpected duties. Our own doctor, 'Stinker' Dowell, an admirable Welshman whose pre-war existence was largely concerned with silicosis and matters to do with miners' lungs, was understandably chary of assisting the French without an interpreter. Called in the middle of the night to an emergency in our village and finding no Henry, he despatched his orderly to wake me up as I could speak a little French. With both apprehension and reluctance I accompanied him to the patient's house, being informed on the way that it looked liked being 'a difficult delivery'. Despite several degrees of frost, I broke into a heavy sweat and was in poorish shape when ushered into the front room of a small cottage occupied, as far as I could see, by about twenty people. This was obviously a public occasion like a royal birth in earlier times. I was greeted warmly and pushed forward, to find poor Stinker also sweating and complaining that he 'couldn't make the buggers understand' (he told me later that he done no midwifery since qualifying).

The expectant mother was lying very calmly on a huge bed flanked by friends and relations. Fortunately one of these was the very agreeable wife of the farmer in whose house we had our mess. I gravitated towards her, and after an interminable torrent of words, not wholly understood, gathered that the local *'sage-femme'* was in attendance but did not like to do anything without permission of the British *accoucheur*.

I said I was sure that the latter would welcome the help of

such an able assistant, told Stinker that he was in real luck, pushed the *sage-femme* forward and made for the door. Here a mountainous man, the brother of the expectant lady, shook me warmly by the hand, gave me a large glass of brandy, coupled with the words 'Nous attendons', and then leant against the longed-for exit.

Fortunately the wait was not long and there were few problems as the lady had previously had several children. More brandy, 'Bruce, what do you say for push?' – 'Poussez, Stinker', ghastly noises, slaps and Heaven knows what, and finally the famous bleat from the child, much emotion and many embraces all round. At one moment I found myself about to kiss Stinker.

When Henry returned the next day he was more than contrite, and when I asked him if he had ever assisted at a childbirth he said 'No', adding the gratuitous information that unfortunately he had no children 'as neither of the two bitches that I was married to wanted to spoil their figures'. As a result of this gynaecological adventure the *sage-femme* mistakenly regarded me as a source of medical assistance and at a later date enlisted my services again – before Stinker could be summoned and when Henry was absent on quite legitimate business. On this occasion the sufferer was Monsieur Chévy, the richest man in the village, a shifty-looking and unpopular person who lived in quite a grand and utterly hideous house. I suspected that most of the villagers were his debtors or mortgagees.

I was inducted into his bedroom and there left alone with him, stretched on his bed in his night shirt, clutching his genitalia and groaning lugubriously. Somewhat shaken I endeavoured to engage him in soothing conversation, praying that Stinker would soon arrive. The scene conjured up one of Zola's more earthy novels and I was very conscious of the contrast between the stuffy and smelly room and the sunlit village street outside, where I could see Ditton, my troop sergeant, cheerfully admonishing some luckless soldier.

After seeming hours the stocky form of Captain Dowell RAMC came through the door. 'Well, Bruce, what's the matter with him?' 'Probably clap,' I diagnosed. 'Well, we'd better give him a catheter.' Once again a heavy sweat broke out on me, but with the doctor's arrival I had averted my eyes from the patient to look out of the window and could see his truck and the orderly now talking to Sergeant Ditton. With a presence of mind that has seldom visited me since, I opened the window and shouted to Ditton to send the orderly up and then removed myself cravenly from this urinary battlefield. Stinker bore me no ill will and later came up to our mess to have a much-needed drink saying that he'd 'given the old bastard a good blow through'.

Later, in the winter, I managed to become stricken with 'flu which developed into mild pleurisy. Stinker was in his element and put in much time listening to my lungs, finally recommending that I needed to recuperate in a warm climate. I had hoped that I might have returned temporarily to England but, before long, I was on the Blue Train en route for Cannes.

Dozy Willis, who would have had friends on Pitcairn Island should a visit have been contemplated there, had long known Lady Trent, widow of the original Jesse Boot, the cash chemist. Part of the year she lived in a handsome villa on the Californie hill, which she and her husband had equipped as an officers' convalescent home in the previous war. She was patriotically prepared to repeat the performance but as events turned out I was to be the only beneficiary of her bounty.

I left Fonquevillers on New Year's Day, lunched with some friends in Paris and boarded the Blue Train in the evening. During dinner I had some desultory conversation with a middle-aged Hungarian lady who spoke tolerable English. I had quite a lot of magazines and papers with me, some of which she asked to borrow, saying that she would return them in the morning. I slept remarkably well until the *wagon lit* attendant called me the next day, bringing in the journals, about which I had forgotten. He gave the rather surprising information that the lady had been removed in the night at Dijon by the French police. I looked carefully through the *Bystander, Horse & Hound* and other unlikely publications for hidden messages, without avail.

Lady Trent's White Russian chauffeur met me at the station in a dark green Rolls-Royce and I moved for ten days into a sybaritic existence. She was a delightful and unaffected person living with her unmarried sister in considerable comfort and served by admirable servants. I was treated far too well, especially as many people seemed to think I had been wounded, despite there being no fighting. Indeed there was a rather embarrassing moment when a young French naval officer and I, as symbols of allied unity, were made to stand on a dais in the Carlton Hotel, at some charity gala, clasping each other by the hand before both national anthems were played. On another occasion, taken to luncheon by Lady T. in the house where Prince Leopold died of haemophilia, I drew as my neighbour the widow of Marshal Joffre, an interesting link with the past. She was, I think, his second wife, a formidably upholstered lady. Luckily I had been informed that 'Papa' had been a great trencherman, so we cruised fairly easily along gastronomic channels.

A retired doctor of the Indian Medical Service and a very social French physician examined my chest rather perfunctorily before lunch one day and agreed that I was sound. Back I went to Fonquevillers, though strangely I have no recollection of the return journey from Cannes.

No sooner had I returned to 'A' Squadron than there was an alert and we moved up for the second time to the Belgian frontier. We were billeted near Roubaix, with our mess in a turreted villa of unbelievable hideousness. However, at least it was warm, a great blessing in that very cold winter, and we made the best of our circumstances with a battalion of the Coldstream Guards as congenial neighbours. We must have stayed there for a week before the alarm subsided and it was during this period that our regimental chaplain preached a sermon of such power ('Be strong and of a good courage') that a couple of troopers and certainly one young officer were obliged to retire from the congregation.

This interesting cleric, the Revd Godfrey Macmanaway, had joined us when we arrived in France. An Ulsterman, currently rector of Londonderry and the son of a former Bishop of Clogher, he had been an airman in the First War and proudly wore RFC wings on his tunic. Extremely convivial, eloquent in the pulpit (he never prepared his sermons), rather idle and immensely social, he was an asset to any assembly, and there was little he did not appear to have done in his life. At a later date we briefly shared quarters and I observed that he invariably had his servant bring him a glass of warm whisky and water before getting up in the morning. He then smoked a powerful pipe before arising to his ablutions and a hearty breakfast. He claimed never to have had a hangover.

Assiduously political, he resigned his living in 1950 when elected to Westminster as Unionist Member for West Belfast. Confusion then arose as to whether he should be permitted to take his seat, since there was doubt about whether the Church of Ireland was disestablished or not. After considerable excitement – I think his case warranted a leading article in *The Times* – he was disqualified. He returned to Belfast in some chagrin and died the following year of a fall or a stroke when leaving the Ulster Club.

A constant feature of my life was Trooper Smallridge who had been assigned to me before the war as first servant. A Welshman from a mining family in Treherbert, Glamorganshire, he was roughly my age, perhaps a little older, a remarkably good driver, small and lithe, with a slight stutter. He made friends wherever he went, from my august grandmother (his youngest sister came to work for her as a housemaid) to the most ill-assorted Arabs.

Before the war he cannot have had too many military duties (officers' servants were the bane of sergeant-majors – they could never get their hands on them for their own purposes), as most of his time must have been taken up in attending to the voluminous wardrobe that was needed for even an ordinary subaltern's life. He came away with me all the winter when I was hunting, cleaning my clothes and boots to a degree of perfection that will never be seen again. He still lives in Treherbert and we correspond and telephone periodically, though he would be appalled if he could see the undisciplined attire in which I am writing these words. Our ways only parted when I was wounded and captured. He soldiered on until after the end of the war, finally leaving the regiment at Villach in Austria sometime in the summer of 1945. He returned then to me for a brief time while I was still in the Army, bringing with him my Everyman copy of Lord Chesterfield's *Letters to His Son,* which had cost about 2/6d when I purchased it in Reigate in 1941. It had travelled with me to the Middle East, was with me throughout the desert campaign and was in my jeep when I was taken prisoner. Smallridge hung on to it for the rest of the war and it went with him through the remainder of the North African campaign and then to Italy. I still possess this battered and much-travelled volume.

Despite the various alarms, life during that particular hard winter and spring was both monotonous and uncertain. Our training was restricted both by geographical boundaries and by a limitation on the use of petrol. Living in close proximity, with not too much to do, was irksome at times, especially for those with a temperament like Andrew Horsburgh-Porter, who was the epitome of the free range officer. Someone coming into the small farmhouse parlour that we used for a squadron mess said that it resembled a scene from *Journey's End,* but 'above ground and without shellfire'! Our only view was that of the midden.

I found myself becoming restless and felt very envious of

Tony Warre who had joined the Hopkinson Mission, one of those private armies that were to proliferate during the coming years. A rather raffish and cosmopolitan affair, it was quartered at Valenciennes and said to be destined for 'special reconnaissance'. Its ambitious little progenitor, 'Hoppy', cast a fly in my direction but any potential interest on my part was firmly squashed by Herbert Lumsden. The Mission, on returning to England after Dunkirk, blossomed into the organisation called Phantom, and Hoppy went on to be an early parachutist commander and was killed or drowned at the Sicilian landings in 1943.

Leave to England had started at the end of 1939, about ten days at a time being granted. Owing to my luxurious convalescence in Cannes, I was held back from this privilege ('never a right', as Captain Ransome so foreseeingly had taught us) until late March. By this time various morale-boosting schemes were in force, one of which was to revive the regimental band. Most of the bandsmen were serving in other regimental capacities, so they had only to be reunited with their instruments for martial music to enliven the drab villages of the Pas de Calais. In consequence each returning leave party, perhaps one or two officers and a dozen troopers, was loaded up at Victoria Station with a selection of trombones and bassoons brought to the terminus by men of the 'details'. As those coming back to France were not at their sunniest at the end of their furloughs, this arrangement had not hitherto proved entirely popular, let alone successful. I was therefore instructed to pay particular attention to my consignment of band instruments which had, I believe, been increased in size. Despite visions of being saddled with the silver kettle drums, I said 'Of course, of course'; and then forgot all about it as I landed in England for ten days of 'madder music and stronger wine'.

During the last of these, when Neil Speke and I had moved, enjoyably but improvidently, into a suite in the Ritz, I discovered that by flying to Paris in the morning and thence taking a train, one could arrive at Arras at the same time as the leave party, who had quitted Victoria the previous evening. One thereby gained an extra day and night. So I was both vexed and disturbed on the point of departure to receive a terse telephone call from the officer in charge of the 'details' saying that the leave party had left Victoria without the band instruments, as I had not been there to take charge and the senior NCO (sensible man) had declined the responsibility.

I boarded the Air France aeroplane with an appalling hangover, the realisation that my overdraft had gone through the ceiling and the anticipation of trouble ahead. The hangover soon evaporated, the overdraft had to await my return from Dunkirk in June (I have an idea that the very nice bank manager read the casualty lists with somewhat mixed feelings), and the trouble duly materialised. I received a well-deserved and unbelievably stinging telling-off from Herbert Lumsden, who confined me to Fonquevillers indefinitely: no visits to Arras, no social calls to other regiments, and various other privations. Fortunately, a further alarm took us to the frontier again. By the time we returned in April the colonel was ordered home awaiting promotion and my sins were forgotten.

By the end of April spring was upon us and it seemed that we would live at Fonquevillers for ever. I had managed to move my sleeping quarters out of the mess into the house of the village schoolmaster, said to be a Communist. He was bearded, always wearing leather leggings, and very civil. Smallridge tucked himself in somewhere and helped to dig the garden. I settled down to a regime of serious reading. It was all very tranquil and even Andrew seemed more relaxed.

As it turned out, he and I were to be the only two original officers of the squadron at the outbreak of hostilities. Others had moved or been posted elsewhere, no doubt to do with our expanding army, and in fact the whole regiment was somewhat different from what it had been seven months before. The colonel had gone, and Rodney Palmer, our second in command, was at home, either on leave or on a course. We had with us on a temporary attachment John Erne, originally an officer in the Blues, who had been recalled at the outbreak of war and eventually assigned to his native North Irish Horse, which was being resuscitated as an armoured car unit. A major, it seemed that he was being groomed to command his regiment and in the meantime had come to us for practical knowledge. I cannot better what Henry de la Falaise wrote of him: 'A keenly attractive-looking Irishman in his middle thirties. Gifted with enormous charm, he was a most likeable character. Extremely quiet and calm, he kept his emotions in control at all times, even under trying conditions. He was my conception of a thorough gentleman, of what an ideal gentleman should be.' The easiest of companions and singularly unselfish, he was indeed a great addition to the squadron. His father had been killed in 1914 and he had succeeded to his grandfather's earldom two months later.

'A' Squadron was also fortunate in having the splendid Sergeant-Major Tree, who was a sort of 'admirable Crichton'. When I joined he was mess sergeant, looking after temperamental chefs and arranging the officers' comforts with both style and skill. He had much of the character of a porter of a London club, tactful, with beautiful manners and the ability to sort out a tricky situation, sometimes with surprisingly ruthless invective. More familiar to us in a tail-coat than in battledress, he appeared to have made an effortless metamorphosis from peace to war.

I commanded No. 1 Troop with Sergeant Ditton as troop sergeant. He was a tremendous athlete and sportsman, with a passion for PT; the amount of exercise that he took each day was prodigious. But all this excessive fitness let him down. When the fighting started he seized up completely after three or four days and had to be sent home (evacuated would not be the right word) with immovable stoppage of the bowels. He was fearfully upset by this and I certainly missed him sorely as he was a most competent and intelligent NCO. He was replaced by Sergeant Lewis who had also been in the officers' mess before the war. Very imperturbable and with the manner of Sergeant-Major Tree, he adapted easily to a more active role and proved a tower of strength.

I had an excellent driver called Morgan and my late groom, Griffiths, as gunner. The former was rather volatile and the latter very stolid, but they got on well together. We also had an especially good man called Cheeseman, a reservist, who later became an NCO. In those days each troop still had two motor-cyclist despatch riders and here I was particularly well served. One of them was another reservist, Trooper Chalk. On finishing his service he became an AA man in Sussex and I often used to see him when he returned to his duties after the war. The other, Sparkes, was an exceptional soldier and became a troop leader in Egypt and Italy and was to receive both the MM and the DCM.

No. 2 Troop was commanded by a most delightful young 11th Hussar, Peter Arkwright. Not much more than twenty, looking even younger, he was a natural soldier of considerable intelligence with a great love of animals and flowers. He had a completely unaffected personality and was loved by his men. No. 3 Troop, normally commanded by Tim Bishop, who was temporarily away on leave, was under the charge of Andrew Roddick who had recently come out from England. The nephew of Herbert Lumsden's wife Elsie, he had the ability to be an outstanding officer, even if his heart was really in farming. He was then still a very young man, but a confirmed bachelor in the making, a member of Arthur's Club with a taste for vintage port. Like his Uncle Herbert, he had both humour and humanity and a permanent twinkle in his eye.

Our transport was looked after by Basil Hall, an erudite and able barrister, who handled the logistic complexities of the coming three weeks with infinite patience and skill. He subsequently became a distinguished Treasury draftsman and was knighted. He and I are the only surviving 'A' Squadron officers.

Tim Bishop I have mentioned and he must have returned to us shortly before 10 May. Andrew Horsbrugh-Porter used two of the squadron headquarters' armoured cars to create a fourth troop and we started with this organisation, although by the end of the month we were reduced to two troops, each of two cars, commanded by Tim and myself.

One of my oldest friends, handsome, trim and elegant, only recently dead, he was a unique character and I doubt if anyone could have fitted him into a category. As a result of parental disagreement he had left Stowe to enlist in the Life Guards, eventually obtaining what was called an 'A' Cadetship to Sandhurst, joining us with several other young officers in the latter part of 1938. Before the war life in the ranks of the Household Cavalry was much as it must have been in Victorian times, with unbelievably rigid discipline and considerable hardship. The hours spent in the cleaning of horses and accoutrements were infinite and Tim used to say that even young soldiers looked twenty years older than they actually were. I think he was lucky in that having a little money he could get a lot of this work done for him by others, but the standards set by the 'Plungers' were those by which he lived, giving a certain old-fashioned austerity to part of his nature.

He could write attractively and was a gifted artist, like his beautiful sister, Molly Scott. All his armoured cars had friezes and frescoes inside them of sporting scenes, and one only wishes they could have been preserved. He was also an effective, sympathetic and polished rider, with a wide knowledge of horses, and in later life became a well-known and respected judge of hunters. I could have wished for no better companion in the hazards ahead of us: blessed with a keen sense of the ridiculous, he was an infallibly competent soldier without any overdoses of enthusiasm. He was to become a most efficient adjutant in the desert.

The following incident may illustrate his character. One very cold day our two troops had to rendezvous on a scheme with the rest of the squadron in the *place* of some depressing mining town like Lens. We both arrived early and entered into conversation with a French artilleryman in charge of five or six saddled horses tethered outside a substantial and sombre house. The animals all had rather long coats, had obviously been ridden hard and had sweated, and were now shivering in the icy wind. We inquired whether his officers, their riders, were at a conference or something similar. 'Non,' came the reply, with a jerk of the thumb, 'au bordel.'

Tim's sketchbook appeared as if by magic. In a flash he had captured the whole scene – the unshaven, pipe-smoking orderly, the quivering, uncomfortable horses and the ugly, discreet, lace-windowed building with its hint of old-fashioned commercial pleasure. Probably I was too complimentary about the sketch, because he immediately found fault with one of the horses and then, very typically, tore up the sheet of paper, and scattered its pieces to the wind.

'B' Squadron was led by William Browne-Clayton, a saturnine officer from County Carlow, Andrew Horsbrugh-Porter's brother-in-law. I think he suffered from some liver complaint which made him somnolent and frequently testy, and with his rather yellow complexion he looked like a Victorian satirical novelist's idea of an Indian Army officer.

'C' Squadron's destinies lay in the hands of Dozy Willis, an idiosyncratic soldier if ever there was one. Dressed almost invariably in an old box-cloth coaching coat that had belonged to his uncle and a red side hat, he treated the enemy and senior officers with an impartial and refreshing lack of respect. His second in command was Rupert Byass, originally a regular, but rejoining us from the reserve of officers after a disastrous first marriage and various financial troubles. Good-looking, rather disreputable, amusing and attractive, he and his second wife Celia (called, not without justification, 'the most dangerous woman in London') might well have graced one of Evelyn Waugh's novels. Both are now dead but they were remarkably good friends to me, though suspected by the more staid of exerting a bad influence.

Rupert and Dozy got on uncommonly well and their curious kind of dual control worked admirably in 'C' Squadron which always had a distinctive character of its own. I have to confess to a special affection for it as I started in it under 'British' Smith (now believed to be at GHQ with a special wireless set as regimental link) and ended up commanding it in the desert. Both the other squadrons had some very high-class troop leaders, notably Peter Miller-Mundy and John Clark-Kennedy in 'B' and Edward Mann and Tatton Brinton in 'C'.

The regiment had also acquired a troop of Sappers from the Royal Monmouthshire Royal Engineers, I believe the only Militia unit remaining in the Army. They were mostly miners from the Forest of Dean, immensely versatile in all aspects of their craft and quite unmoved under fire. We were going to owe a lot to them and to their able and courageous commander, a subaltern called David Smith.

Our armoured cars were burdened with extra bits and pieces, such as Union Jacks to wave at unsure allies, rolls of Dennert wire for creating road blocks, canisters of mysterious chemicals for raising smoke screens and other 'white knight' devices, and, to crown all, carrier pigeons in case the radio failed. Each troop was provided with a pair, which were delivered in neat baskets as we moved off on 10 May. Their home was in Lille, presumably a sort of avian intelligence centre, but by the time we released them the place was in German hands. So the poor things were probably pressed into enemy service.

Encounter

FRANCE – BELGIUM : MAY – JUNE 1940

The seven months prior to the Blitz passed very much the same for us as they did for any other British troops then in France. We did a lot of useful training and gained some knowledge of the role we were to play if and when the campaign opened. Some practical experience of this was obtained in three scares (in November 1939 and in January and April 1940) when we moved up to the Belgian frontier, prepared to cross over.

The Allied strategy has been frequently explained and by people considerably more qualified than I, and I repeat it now only in so far as it affected ourselves. The BEF, with the French 1st Army on its right, was to advance to the line of the River Dyle where it was expected to make contact with the enemy and thereafter fight a delaying action. The French 1st Army was to have the 3ème Division Légère Mecanisée in front as a protective screen, with whose left the 12th Lancers were to be in touch, while our own left was in the neighbourhood of Malines. The classic simplicity of this plan appeared to be rather marred by the question of the unknown future actions of the Belgian Army. It will be remembered that Belgium preserved strict neutrality until the German invasion of the Low Countries on 10 May. The plans for the BEF changed periodically but the Dyle plan was the final one. I remember, at some period prior to its adoption, being greatly thrilled at the thought that when hostilities opened my task was to rush to Mons and seize the telephone exchange. We studied the map most assiduously for this. 'A' Squadron, commanded by Andrew Horsbrugh-Porter (I was a troop leader in this squadron), was to cross the frontier near

Roubaix and move to the east of the Dyle where it would fan out and make contact with the 3ème DLM on its right and with 'C' Squadron (Dozy Willis) on its left. Our first squadron HQ was to be at a village called Grez Doiceau, between Wavre and Jodoigne and my troop (No. 1) was to contact the French.

When the German entry into the Low Countries did take place, it happened very suddenly and we received no warning. We had returned to our billets near Arras on 9 May, having been away on a scheme with the Hopkinson Mission at Valenciennes. At that time no state of emergency existed (i.e. notice to move at from one to four hours' notice), though this had been the rule on previous scares.

On the morning of 10 May Smallridge came to call me saying that he had just heard on the wireless that the Germans had entered Holland that morning, but that as yet no orders had come for the regiment. I walked up to the mess for breakfast and while I was there a message came from RHQ saying that we were at short notice to move.

While Andrew was giving the necessary orders another message arrived telling us to move to the frontier immediately. We moved by troops, independently, shortly after this, leaving the transport to come on later under regimental arrangements. So far I had hardly had time to think; now I began to wonder what was going to happen. Everything seemed so very normal as we took the familiar road to Arras. It was a lovely fresh morning and I thought rather enviously of the French peasants that we passed, busy on their farms and undisturbed by the clamour of European wars. Ten days later these same peasants were joining the streams of refugess fleeing westwards from Arras.

In the town itself there was a certain superficial excitement and much *va et vient* of staff cars. Outside 'Etbts Julien Damoy', where I used to buy a lot of food for the mess, the manager and all his assistants were chattering wildly. I shouted to them and the old man immediately threw me a large box of dates which Griffiths, my gunner, caught. The dates were followed by many benedictions – I felt very impolite rushing on when all my previous transactions with that establishment had been conducted in a flood of Gallic loquacity; but no doubt the manager, as a veteran of *'quatorze'*, understood the rigours of war.

I reached Lannoy on the frontier (it was on the main Roubaix–Tournai road) about 11.30 a.m. and by noon all the squadron had arrived. We were told that we were to cross at 1 p.m. and move as previously arranged to Grez Doiceau. Tim Bishop and I went and sat in a little garden where he produced a bottle of Moët & Chandon. With this and some bread and ham we made an excellent luncheon, while indulging in rather fantastic speculation about the future.

At 1 p.m. the *douaniers* lifted the barriers and we moved into Belgium on that well-memorised route: Tournai-Ath-Enghien-Wavre-Grez Doiceau. My troop was leading. In Tournai itself we were received with wild acclaim by the populace who threw us flowers and made the most flattering remarks about the British Army. The whole enterprise began to have something of the air of a musical comedy – an illusion that was only to last a day.

I was still feeling rather lyrical when we got onto the Ath road. It was the most perfect afternoon and the country looked wonderfully green, with the early flowers in profusion. Griffiths brought me up short by pointing skywards and there I saw fifteen to twenty German bombers flying westwards, very high and in perfect formation. It was the first time that I had seen those black crosses and they seemed menacingly ominous.

There was little traffic on the road except a small but steady westbound stream of expensive cars, most of them crammed with luggage and people. I remember being very galled when a staff car followed by two military policemen on motor-cycles overtook us. I had been living in the proud belief that we were the first troops into Belgium and now we were being passed by some nonentity of an assistant provost marshal! I consoled myself with the thought that things must be fairly safe if he could rush ahead so impetuously.

We halted for a time by a lake in the Forêt de Soignes, in the most idyllic surroundings. There was some ack-ack fire a long way distant but people were quite happy driving slowly round the forest roads taking the afternoon air. Two American girls came up and gave us some chocolate and marrons glacés. They said they were leaving Brussels the next morning on the advice of their consul. They had been skiing earlier on, whether in Austria or Switzerland I do not recall, and had been touring through Bavaria and down the Rhine. It says much for American neutrality that they were, apparently, able to travel through the assembling German armies. They seemed hardly aware that hostilities had started.

The last lap of the journey was rather hampered by the greater part of the Belgian Army who seemed to be going in all directions, very gay and festive with most of their vehicles and horses adorned with large bunches of white lilac. It was in bloom everywhere and remains one of my most powerful memories of that May.

We reached Grez Doiceau in the evening and I was sent on into Jodoigne to see if anything was happening there. The people were standing about outside their houses but the only troops I saw were a few Belgian soldiers. No one knew very much – a foretaste of things to come – though there was a rumour of fighting near Liège. I returned halfway to Grez Doiceau and stopped on a ridge overlooking Jodoigne. While we were eating our supper (eggs mysteriously appeared, as they frequently did) masses of French armoured troops belonging to the 3ème DLM passed us. Andrew spoke to me on the wireless but had no new orders. He came up himself a little later with Henry de la Falaise who had just returned from leave by some adroit lorry-hopping. Henry said Paris was quiet 'and very beautiful'. Andrew thought we were to link up with the French early in the morning. The other squadrons were all in position. The one that had gone through Brussels had received a tremendous ovation. Andrew also reported that the colonel had rejoined us, having flown from England that morning.

Nothing much happened during the night except that we heard considerable heavy bombing. Very early in the morning (11 May) I moved out to contact 3ème DLM in the neighbourhood of St Trond. Squadron HQ moved to near Tirlemont while the remaining troops took up positions on the River Gette which runs north and south through Tirlemont and to Jodoigne. Just after passing through Tirlemont my troop was spotted by a German reconnaissance plane and about ten minutes later we were visited by four dive bombers. I made what use I could of a few trees and the shadows of houses but we must have been very conspicuous as we were the only traffic moving east on a straight white road. In the course of that journey they came after us three separate times and I never enjoyed anything less in my life. One or two bombs dropped unpleasantly close and one of the cars was lifted clean off the road though with no worse harm than losing the use of its wireless set. By far the greatest damage was done among the unfortunate refugees who thronged the sides of the road.

Halfway to St Trond it became apparent that large numbers of Belgian troops were drifting westwards, in not much sort of order. None of them seemed anxious to stop or to give any coherent information. Eventually I located the general commanding 7th Belgian Division, standing with his staff outside a small *estaminet*. He had just had the 'overs' from our bombs and his entourage seemed rather shaken. He said that there had been some kind of action near Maastricht and that the Belgian Army was withdrawing westwards, rapidly. I found the latter piece of information superfluous.

I liked the situation less and less but resolved to push on to St Trond. The road was now fairly congested and the German bombers had attacked the refugees again with the most lamentable results. I could not help feeling it strange that the first dead one saw were women and children but I was beginning to realise that my ideas of war were a trifle old-fashioned; the truth upset my knightly preconceptions. St Trond we approached most cautiously as there was firing going on in the town. (St Trond is only about fifty miles from Aachen. I cherish the possibility that my troop went further east than any other unit of the BEF.) Luckily I found a traffic policeman of the 12ème Cuirassiers outside who took me to one of their officers, a most engaging person who told me that there was a dogfight going on in the town between French and German armoured elements.

We went forward and had a look at this together from a safe distance. On the way back he produced a pair of enormous clippers or tongs, veterinary in appearance, which he assured me he would use for a useful physiological purpose on any German he met. It seems unfortunate, in the light of later events, that more of the French Army were not infeected by his eugenic enthusiasm.

I was about to send off all my information by wireless but discovered that more bombing had put my only remaining set out of action. So I sent off Sparkes, one of my despatch riders. He got back to Andrew Porter wonderfully quickly, riding through Tirlemont in the midst of a dive-bombing attack, and was back within the hour with orders for me to return to squadron HQ. Our journey back down that unpleasant road was, thankfully, without much incident but we arrived at HQ in time for a fresh air attack. We were there long enough for the wireless to be put in order and then went off to contact 3ème DLM headquarters. I was told to stay there and we managed to get an hour or two of sleep before being sent to watch the St Trond road again. At dawn I was sent to look for a pilot who had been shot down near St Trond but I discovered that the French had already rescued him and sent him to the rear.

This was the last we saw of that much-hated road. During

that day (12 May) the Germans reached the Gette where they were held up by blown bridges and, in one sector, by the Belgians. We spent the day watching in case there was a breakthrough. There was constant shooting along the river banks. At one moment I was put under arrest by a Belgian colonel who asked me to take my cars through what he said was a ford and attack at least a German battalion – while he no doubt applauded. A few enemy shells sent him to cover and me out of arrest.

That night was not one for sleep as the sky was full of planes. Heavy firing continued and the Belgians kept anticipating ugly events by saying the Germans were crossing the river in collapsible boats and large numbers. In order to maintain touch I had to keep visiting three or four different Belgian HQs, a hair-raising business as few of their sentries could speak French and all were very quick on the trigger.

The following day the fighting became hotter although there was not too much for us to do. The colonel came up with Andrew and told me to expect an order to withdraw later in the day as it was anticipated that the enemy might break through on either bank. There was endless aerial activity and Tirlemont was repeatedly dive-bombed.

Soon after dark I was told to rendezvous at a village a few miles east of Louvain. Peter Arkwright's troop was only a mile or two from me so we joined forces and travelled together. We had to go by secondary roads and these were all hideously blocked by Belgian troops and refugees, whose morale was not improved by the continual and indiscriminate dropping of bombs and flares. Nor did it help to be using maps which had the place names in French when all the signposts were in Flemish. It was a nightmare journey made worse by an insidious sleepiness against which one had to fight the whole time. My troop were wonderful, never complaining and receiving with the utmost equanimity the completely undeserved maledictions I frequently bestowed upon them in extenuation of my own errors. I do not suppose the distance was more than twenty miles on the map but we must have done fully double that by the time we had made detours to avoid blocks. It was dawn before we reached the rendezvous and could take up new positions south east of Louvain. Here, strangely enough, the roads were quite empty of refugees. It was a very hot morning and a stilly silence hung over the countryside.

Later we were relieved by some troops of the 15th/19th Hussars and moved back to squadron HQ on the outskirts of Louvain. On the way there my troop was singled out for a strafing attack from an enemy fighter but at that period the Germans were not using armour-piercing bullets and we only collected a few honourable dents on the plating. I found Andrew in conference with Donald Frazer, the CO of the 15th/19th – I little thought that the next time I saw him would be in a German prison camp two and a half years later – but John Erne, our second in command, said that we were going back for a few days' rest. This was a welcome piece of news as we had only had two or three hours' sleep in the last ninety-six. Poor John had been stung on the eyelid by a wasp and was suffering agonies.

The squadron was collected about 2 p.m. and we moved off through Louvain to cross the Dyle. To reach the bridge of boats we had to go by the most circuitous route and I was terrified that I should lead the whole squadron into a dead end. We arrived there eventually and found the river bank manned by the Grenadiers, all looking immaculate. I shouted out to a friend of mine and wondered why he was so slow in recognising me until I realised that we were all covered with dirt, unshaven and looking like nothing on earth. We crossed the bridge of boats (all the others had been blown) and moved off to a 'harbour' which was somewhere in the Forêt de Soignes, south of Brussels. We found there that our transport, who were always miraculously in the right place, had food and billets ready and had even found time to catch a couple of fifth columnists. It seemed unlikely that we would have anything to do until the following day and we all went to sleep at about 7 p.m. after a wonderful meal. Tim and I slept in an enormous voluptuous bed in a very attractive little house that, we imagined, belonged to some *poule de luxe;* we hardly woke when a German aeroplane was shot down and crashed a few hundred yards away. But we were aroused early with the information that the squadron had a special task and had to move at once to Lennick St Martin where GHQ then was.

Our mess cook was just getting ready a gargantuan breakfast and it nearly broke his heart having to pack everything up. I scalded my mouth with boiling coffee and mounted my car with a large and messy piece of bread and honey. Lennick St Martin was south west of Brussels and Lord Gort and his staff were in a small house off the *place*. Apparently fifth columnists had been causing a lot of trouble and we had to provide a protective ring round the town so as to regulate the flow of unlicensed wanderers. There was a constant stream of traffic moving through and it was difficult to do much about it. We were bombed once or twice but otherwise little happened. The night passed rather jumpily. Tim Bishop was sent off to arrest the burgomaster who was thought to have pro-Nazi leanings and to be the prospective gauleiter. He had wisely disappeared and Tim and his men had a cheerless vigil in his garden.

In the morning (16 May) we were sent off to some infantry brigade who were approachng to defend a southern bulge south east of Hal in the area Braine Le Château - Waterloo. The squadron was strung out along a railway line covering a front of ten miles or so. This was really too much to watch with only three troops, especially as it involved a lot of bridges. My troop was in Braine itself where there was a large road bridge over the railway cutting.

About 3 or 4 p.m. a truck of our attached Sappers arrived to join me and I received orders to blow up the bridge as a German advance was shortly expected. The town was full of refugees and French troops and I could see it would be a job to clear them out. I hoped, perhaps ingenuously, that by the time the bridge was ready for demolition they would have moved on. Johnson, the RE sergeant, worked with the agility of a monkey as he swung about on a rope, above a thirty-foot drop, knocking holes in the masonry. When the bridge was ready to be blown up, Braine was still very full of people and transport; in fact it was a worse mêlée than before. A seemingly endless column of lorries was passing over the bridge, while French gunners and cavalry were now added to the diverse elements in the streets. I felt rather desperate about the whole thing. Even shouting 'Je ferai sauter le pont en trois minutes exactement' had singularly little effect and I reflected that the French had much of that phlegm which they so frequently attribute to the British. The jam only began to shift when we started to lead out individual horses which we despatched up the road with a good 'belt', irrespective of their riders' wishes. The troop enjoyed this enormously and Griffiths, who had been my groom before the war, showed a splendid impartiality, at one moment accelerating the departure of a speechless major and the next that of a whole gun team. In this manner we succeeded in clearing the town of Braine in about forty minutes. The bridge was at last clear of traffic and the fuse was lit. I had a gripping fear that vehicles would arrive on it at the crucial moment but it went up without loss of life. Unfortunately the explosion only cratered the road and it was still possible to cross over. Johnson started to put in more charges but I received orders to retire north west of Braine onto some high ground on the main Hal road. I gathered that we had to cover the withdrawal of the infantry.

I was joined in my new position by Tim with a makeshift troop of two squadron HQ cars. The REs laid a land mine in the road in front of us and behind this we awaited the enemy who, we were assured, might arrive any minute. A very silent night descended upon us. About 9 p.m. we heard what we thought was motor traffic coming up the hill out of Braine and a few minutes later the land mine exploded with what seemed a world-shattering detonation and then someone gave a shout. In the momentary glare we had been able to see a vehicle or two and promptly opened fire on them; evidently with great effect as they appeared to stop immediately. We gave them another burst or two, without any retaliation, and after a few minutes of rather frenzied conference moved down the road in our cars, very gingerly, to investigate. I did not like it at all, nor did Tim. We thought some very unpleasant trap lay ahead. I kept drinking from my water bottle, which I believe is a sure sign of fear.

On the far side of the mine's crater was a dark shape. Then we heard a rustling noise at the side of the road. I switched my torch in that direction and saw emerge from the ditch two figures with their hands up. As they approached I saw they were a French colonel and his driver. It was a rather disastrous anticlimax. I endeavoured to apologise but the colonel took it very well considering that his car was riddled with bullets which he and his companion had only evaded by abandoning ship in the nick of time. His unfortunate despatch rider who was preceding him had been blown up by the mine. We found his body later and felt very bad about it. I sent the colonel and his man back to squadron HQ and then talked to Andrew on the wireless. He said that very high authority was still of the opinion that the enemy would be upon us shortly. I ventured to take a contrary view and said I was convinced that a considerable part of the French Army lay between us and the Germans. He was inclined to agree with me and I was proved correct in about half an hour's time when a procession of French transport started passing us. Most of it belonged to one of the Divisions Marocaines and was drawn by grey horses which I thought looked a trifle out of date. They took most of the night to pass and it was dawn before the road was free for the enemy. It was still free when we withdrew to Hal in the morning.

It is at this point that my memory is none too good, dislocated, I suppose, by sheer lack of sleep. The BEF was withdrawing to the French frontier (Gort line) and we had the task of covering part of this withdrawal. We had two nights and three days with hardly any sleep and I find that I can only recall a few isolated scenes.

I do remember at one place (Lessines) looking through my glasses over the river and seeing a solid mass of German troops – at first I thought it was an illusion. On another occasion I met a battalion of some Highland regiment whose transport had not arrived and who were marching along the road grey-faced with fatigue, having not stopped for two or three days. I had often heard of people falling asleep on the march in the First World War and now I saw it happening in reality. And one day I encountered Wilfred Davies, a major in the 13th/18th Hussars, when we were both having trouble with enemy anti-tank guns. He was, as ever, full of good spirits. He was another friend I was next to meet in 1943 in Spangenberg.

The air of desertion that hung over the country was rather sinister. The farms were often abandoned and the air was full of the sound of unfed beasts. The cows were particularly piteous, wandering hopelessly about with distended udders. One of my troop was an adept at milking and whenever we stopped he usually succeeded in collecting a pail of fresh milk. The Luftwaffe was as omnipresent as ever during those few days and I saw for the first time a Fiesler Storch which flew over a hedge to look at us and was off again before we could fire a shot.

We finally reached Tournai on 19 May. It had been very badly bombed and presented an appalling contrast to the sunny city of only nine days before – though so much had happened in those nine days that I would not have been surprised if it had completely disappeared. We had to make a considerable detour to reach the only standing bridge over the Escaut.

That evening the regiment was concentrated outside Orchies (near Douai) and we hoped that we might get a little rest as our own particular task appeared to be completed. We were quite unaware of the German breakthrough at Sedan a day or two before. That night we were billeted in a large villa and farm with all the cars parked under the cover of an apple orchard. We managed to get a good night's sleep (for most of us only the second since the beginning of hostilities) but about 7.30 a.m. the next morning Andrew was called to RHQ and we prepared to move.

GHQ was worried now about the area Arras - Cambrai - Péronne - Doullens, where it was suspected that there was considerable fifth column activity as many telephone lines had been cut and it was out of touch with certain outlying units. The regiment was ordered into this area to 'clarify' the situation. We were not told anything about the breakthrough so I presume GHQ was then unaware of the depth of the German thrust towards the coast.

'A' Squadron was ordered to reconnoitre the country south and south west of the main Arras - St Pol road and one troop, mine, was to push on to Doullens to get in touch with 36 Infantry Brigade, with whom there was no communication. We did not reach the Arras - St Pol road until the afternoon as the refugees in the dense mining district round Lens and Vimy made our journey a very slow one. When we finally arrived there we found that the road itself was also packed with refugees – people whose means of transport varied from expensive limousines to their feet and whose common force of propulsion was blind fear. The country south of the road we knew well as it was our former billeting area. This was lucky as it was here that we 'bumped' the northernmost elements of the enemy drive to the coast. 'B' Squadron on our left located considerable tank forces in the Forêt de Beaufort and the troop on my immediate left – Peter Arkwright's – encountered a strong formation in Avesnes le Comte. He had one man killed and a couple wounded but managed to extricate them very gallantly and without further damage.

At the precise moment that I overheard all this on the wireless, my other car (I only had two by now) elected to have a petrol stoppage. We were at a fork road, whose two prongs were divided by a space like a village green. While the crew were trying to clear the stoppage a large column of enemy lorries and armoured cars came down the other road going north west. So I was in an ideal position to shoot them up but could not do so as my 'lame' car prevented a quick getaway. They did not appear to see us and I still hoped to avoid sacrificing the car. The column passed but was rapidly followed by another with more armour in it. This one spotted us and I was compelled to abandon and set fire to one car and beat a hasty and inglorious retreat with eight men in the other. Some of the enemy AFVs chased us but I was able to give them the slip, thanks to a superior knowledge of the district. Even so, it was what the Regency bucks called 'a nice thing'.

The squadron had rendezvoused north of the main road and we took up positions overlooking it to observe the enemy if he should turn in that direction. We had a reasonably peaceful night, apart from alarmist reports brought in by agitated civilians, and early on the following morning (21 May) we concentrated near Arras as we were going to be used in a counter-attack, possibly by 50th Division, on the flank of the German thrust. Our role was suspiciously vague and amounted in fact to that of a suicide squad. We were vastly relieved when we heard we were not required. In the early afternoon we moved back towards the high ground which we had previously occupied. On the way we had a very fierce aerial attack. Squadron HQ suffered rather badly and the signals sergeant was killed by Andrew's side.

Peter Arkwright's troop had the misfortune to run into a wandering German patrol. Two of his men were killed and he himself was very badly wounded. His troop corporal,

Chorley, put up a very fine performance – for which he was subsequently decorated – and managed to get him out and back to HQ. Poor Peter was taken to a dressing station near Lens which unfortunately later fell into enemy hands and he himself died of his wounds shortly after, a tragic loss to everyone. He was only twenty and a most charming person.

We took up our old positions without much else happening and that evening went back to Festubert for the night. I got caught up with a French tank regiment whose colonel reckoned I was a suspicious character and would not let me go for two hours. As a result of this the whole squadron was kept waiting and we did not reach Festubert until the small hours.

The following dawn found us on Vimy Ridge looking south west. The whole situation was becoming rather confused and began distinctly to smell. French troops were withdrawing without, it seemed, any very methodical plan. As far as I can remember we spent that evening operating round Bailleul and the La Bassée Canal, though nothing much occurred and we withdrew again for a few hours to Festubert.

The colonel was very uneasy about the west and was convinced that the enemy was now about to advance from that direction to take the BEF in the rear. The squadron therefore moved off early on 23 May on a long-distance reconnaissance to Hazebrouck and St Omer. It was to be our most unlucky day of the war. We passed through all the back areas of the BEF with everything seeming peaceful; there were no refugees, no German aeroplanes. We were now reduced to three troops of two cars each. We passed through Hazebrouck (where rear GHQ was) and, spreading out, moved towards St Omer with the main road as our axis. Just beyond a village called Renescure we encountered various enemy armoured forces, at the moment stationary but obviously on their way eastwards. Unfortunately we had been unable to see that these had been preceded by infantry who were filtering through the wooded country on either side of the road. These engaged us from the flanks with calamitous results. Poor Andrew Roddick, No. 3 troop leader, was killed and squadron HQ was also attacked, receiving three or four casualties, including John Erne who afterwards died of wounds. I missed most of this as I had been sent off to help an agitated RE major whose company was in an isolated château outside Renescure. We extricated them all quickly, under the noses of four German tanks who failed to see us. I gave the Sappers a few minutes' grace in which to get away and then followed. As luck would have it, we were seen by the enemy infantry in the woods who opened up with everything they had, including anti-tank guns. We tore down the road out of Renescure, brilliantly covered by Sergeant Lewis, now commanding a troop, and reached safety without being badly hit.

We then re-formed outside Hazebrouck. Our information which had been gained at such grievous expense was of great importance as no one had any idea that the enemy were in that area. The resultant rapid move of rear GHQ from Hazebrouck was our only laugh that day. In the evening we moved back to Seclin, near Lille, and rejoined the rest of the regiment.

Next morning we moved to Bois Grenier where we had some rest. It was here that we first heard some official mention of evacuation. The few of us remaining in the squadron were very depressed and I shall never forget the wonderful efforts of Henry de la Falaise to make us laugh with his stories about the involved domestic troubles of the Hollywood stars.

We then spent two days in the area of Ypres and Poperinghe, whose macabre memories were not very inspiring, watching eastwards in the direction of Menin, in conjunction with 8ème Cuirassiers (armoured cars) whom we knew well. Ypres itself was deserted. The Menin Gate had been damaged by bombs. I went into a burnt out shop which had once housed battlefield souvenirs (made in Birmingham) – and found the association of ideas did not really bear thinking about.

On 25 May I was sent off on a long mission to Belgian GHQ, which had disappeared. In approaching a town called Ingelmunster we were fired upon and two ill-placed civilians standing by the roadside were wounded. I worked round to enter the town by another route. As I had expected, it was only held by Belgians. On asking their commanding officer if he had any information, he said among other things, 'Il y a trente minutes, on a fait reculer, *avec célérité,* des auto-mitrailleuses allemandes.' I left him in this heroic belief and went on my way *avec célérité*. In the evening I at length located GHQ but by this time no one was interested as Belgium had either capitulated or was about to do so. I did not return to the squadron till very late.

The next day was spent in watching the reactions of the Belgians after they had ceased fighting. We now had only two troops left in the squadron, each of two cars, and we were kept very busy. I had to go off on a long trip to Roulers and Thourout and I found all the Belgians very uncommunicative. In the former place I had a discussion with the burgomaster who kept breaking into Flemish, which made conversation very difficult, and pointing at the statue of Nurse Cavell which adorns the centre of that town. Finally he made me the symbolic gift of an apple and I was left in some doubt of the whole affair. This sounds highly irrelevant now but one engaged in some strange interviews in quest of information. I began to have less and less idea of what was happening – save that the Germans were doing rather well.

Our last two days as an active unit were spent in some very involved operations round Furnes and Dixmude, blowing up bridges over the Albert Canal and its tributary arms. At a village called Schoorbacke I was responsible for the destruction of an enormous iron swing bridge. I was told this was mined and to hurry up. There was a French Sapper sergeant in charge who refused to blow it up or divulge where the fuses were, despite my assurance of the imminent approach of the enemy – which I knew, this time, for certain. Other bridges on my right and left were going up with encouraging explosions and I was peremptorily asked what I was doing. A brandished revolver and my entire stock of French invective had no effect on my friend and he only operated after I had been compelled to use third degree methods on him. It was hardly the way to treat one's ally; but the bridge disintegrated with the most stupendous noise and bits of it continued falling for some time. Luckily it had been mined properly and it completely disappeared. Only a few minutes later German armoured cars and tanks appeared on the opposite bank and under their spirited fire we withdrew.

That night (28–29 May) we had an unpleasant time in Furnes and the 29th saw most of the regiment on the edge of the Dunkirk perimeter. About midday we withdrew again. I got landed with the job of controlling traffic and sorting French and British into separate streams, which was exasperating work under a considerable aerial bombardment. In the evening the remainder of the squadron concentrated and a little later we received orders to destroy our vehicles. This we did by firing anti-tank bullets into the engines and then pushing the cars into one of the canals. We then marched off with our weapons to a field where we met the remainder of the regiment and the transport. We had some food and collected what kit we could carry and managed to get a comparatively good night's sleep which was sorely needed. Before dawn we were marching off to the seaside town of La Panne, leaving our lorries and spare baggage blazing behind us.

The journey to La Panne was rather arduous as we had a lot of arms and ammunition to carry and most of the men were still very tired. They played up wonderfully and we reached the town by midday. A very exhausting twenty-four hours followed as the regiment was made responsible for policing the beach and assisting in embarkation. Three jetties had been formed of lorries which were driven out into the sea and from the ends of these men were put into rowing boats which took them out to the vessels lying in deeper water. Each squadron had a jetty to look after and we worked, by shifts, until noon of the 31st. Most of the night was spent in getting off walking wounded; by dawn we were embarking ordinary personnel. For the most part discipline was excellent though there were one or two cases which brought little credit to the British Army. There was practically continuous bombing but we had quite a good anti-aircraft barrage, both from the shore and from destroyers, and I saw quite a few of the enemy shot down.

For our embarkation duties all of our officers were made ESOs (embarkation staff officers) and we were given powers to regulate the flow of troops. I think most of us managed to extract a lot of amusement out of a painful situation, by retarding the somewhat headlong rush of one or two staff officers whose duties apparently required their immediate presence in England. We were assisted by four subalterns of the Coldstream who had been sent over from England on the previous day with instructions not to return until everyone got off safely – I fancy they all felt a touch old-fashioned about this.

At midday on 31 May we were relieved by troops of General Alexander's 1st Division and prepared to take our place in the embarkation queue. Unfortunately the Germans chose that moment to start shelling La Panne, causing some casualties among the ships, and the Navy rightly decided to discontinue taking off troops there. We were therefore ordered to march to Dunkirk where apparently there was a 'chance' of getting a passage home. It was a trek of some eight miles along the sand and was really rather trying under considerable bombing and a hot sun. We adopted 'artillery formation' (memories of OTC field days!) and escaped with only a couple of men wounded.

On the outskirts of Dunkirk we met the colonel who had, by some remarkable process, acquired shipping space on two or three cement ships. Into these we gradually embarked, the shorter men having a very watery time as we had to wade out a fair distance. By about 7 p.m. we had all left the shore in some kind of vessel and I then saw the colonel, still looking immaculate, entering a small boat.

I remember very little of the journey back. Someone gave me some rum and I went to sleep in a sort of wheel house, into which we thrust ourselves, although it was already full. I had terrible attacks of cramp during the night and Rupert Byass told me afterwards that I kept kicking some luckless Frenchman in the face and murmuring 'S'il vous plaît, monsieur . . . ' He also told me that the ship was commanded by a midshipman who looked about twelve, assisted by a boatswain aged eighty.

We landed at Margate around 10 a.m. on 1 June.

Intermission

Margate on a beautiful, but perhaps not glorious, First of June was a miracle of organised chaos: some administrative genius had done his work most thoroughly. I note from a telegram which I still possess, sent to my mother, that we must have landed soon after ten o'clock. There was little regimental cohesion as we had all embarked at Dunkirk on various ships, some of which docked at different ports. At least we knew that all our own troops had got away on some sort of vessel, though where they were at the moment, Heaven alone knew. I was worried about the faithful Smallridge, last seen in watery circumstances, but I assumed he would eventually turn up.

Seemingly innumerable trains awaited the stricken army, which primed once more with 'proper' English tea, provided by the Salvation Army and local organisations, was soon being dispersed all over the kingdom. Rupert Byass, Tim and I had a compartment to ourselves and promptly dropped into heavy slumber. We were conscious of the train having stopped at the London Olympia station, but it had started again while we were thinking of getting out and we were carried on to Bletchley through a comfortable, sunlit afternoon.

At Bletchley there were charming ladies awaiting us with reinforcements of tea and cigarettes. I set off to find the RTO in charge to enquire our destination, but was rebuffed brusquely for breaching security: 'Don't you realise there's a war on?' I returned to my companions only to discover that Tim, with more enterprise, had consulted the engine driver who divulged that the train was bound for Warrington in Lancashire. We felt it somewhat unnecessary to travel there before being sent south again and with the help of the station master, a most courteous official, were inducted into a London-bound express and by the time of what Verlaine described as *'l'heure verte'* had been taken by Rupert to White's Club, whose portals can probably have never seen three dirtier guests. This I recall quite vividly but have absolutely no idea how I reached the house which my mother and stepfather inhabited at Tadworth near Reigate, where my grandmother was also in residence. Here I eventually retired to bed and slept for some thirty-six hours, something I have never done since.

It had been a chastening experience. France had collapsed in a manner reminiscent of 1870. England had suffered one of the worst defeats in its history, with a particularly appalling loss of equipment, and the British, paradoxically, thanks to Winston Churchill, the weather and general relief at the 'miracle' of Dunkirk, were in the best of spirits. At that time of my life I had an intense, and probably irrational, admiration for all things French-style, literature, the beauty of the country, paintings, architecture and so on. This admiration had been in no way diminished by the quality of those elite formations with which we had been associated, proper paladins in the great martial tradition. But it was tarnished in the latter days of the retreat when we encountered elements possibly of treason and certainly of 'Don't give a damn'. Ill-equipped, and sadly and badly led by elderly officers, the Reserve and Territorial divisions of the French Army presented a melancholy spectacle. I have a poignant memory, just before Dunkirk, of a transport echelon abandoning their horse-drawn wagons, hardly bothering to release the wretched animals, and wandering away whistling in unison, quite beautifully, 'Tristesse', a then popular tune based on one of Chopin's Etudes.

The BEF was by no means above reproach. It was only a partially professional army, a lot of its equipment was indifferent (thanks to hasty rearmament), and many of its senior officers were too old and too influenced by the tactics of the previous war. They did not have the flexibility to adapt to blitzkrieg methods unless blessed with the imagination and flair of such figures as Alan Brooke, Alexander, Montgomery, Herbert Lumsden and others. The spirit and the courage of the troops was good, and was very good in some regiments, but there seems little doubt that the preservation of the BEF owes much, if not everything, to its very underrated, possibly unimaginative, but totally devoted and heroic commander Lord Gort. It is interesting that a rather self-effacing personality, eschewing all forms of 'P.R.', was able to communicate a feeling of confidence to his troops without having become a public figure.

In the past, engagements were fought in small areas and generals maintained a physical presence as they rode hither and thither on the field of battle which obviously helped to inspire their men. But to transmit inspiration and a link of faith and courage seems to me a gift rather than a technique; and a very remarkable one when it is done by remote control.

I met Gort but once, when given tea at the mess of the Château de Harbarcq, near Arras, which was his pre-Blitz headquarters, by Christopher Jeffreys, one of his ADCs, later to be killed. The general was not very sociable but we shook hands and he said 'I hope you will look after us' and, as far as I remember, nothing else.

However, I presume we did, as he subsequently wrote in his despatches that without the 12th Lancers only a small part of the army would have reached Dunkirk, and within twelve days of reaching England he had awarded the regiment some dozen decorations with an added Military Cross to the gallant Smith of the Monmouthshire Sappers.

It was gratifying to receive congratulations and to know that we had done as well as we could, but after the initial euphoria the more recent memories came flooding back: the speed of modern warfare, the plight of the refugees, the horror of the continual air attacks, the crucifying lack of sleep and, particularly in our squadron, the thought of those who had been killed; and also the moments of sheer unadulterated fear, especially in those periods of silent watching when you were waiting for something to happen.

Emerging from my coma at home, I discovered by telephoning a few friends that the regiment was said to be collecting itself 'somewhere in Dorset'. So I begged a lift to London where I could get more uniform and information. Everything had been abandoned on the other side and I had returned, like most other people, fairly sparsely accoutred.

London really was the hub of the Empire in those days, and news could be obtained astonishingly easily from friends and acquaintances encountered, with seeming frequency, walking the streets of the West End. I met the colonel in the regimental tailors and he informed me that we were reforming at a rather stark camp at Hamworthy, near Poole. 'Probably we can revive the band, as thanks to your foresight most of the instruments are still in England.'

In Piccadilly, a little later, I ran into Henry de la Falaise who had been housed for the past few days in the Cavalry Club. One had hardly had time then to realise the problems of Frenchmen stranded in England, but he assured me that he was going back to collect his Emmita, who had, I think, a Spanish passport, and they were then going to move on somewhere. I said I thought the return voyage might be difficult but he assured me that he was seeing 'that bastard Joe Kennedy' that afternoon. 'America is neutral, he owes a lot to me and I shall get my papers.' Indeed he did and eventually landed up with Emmita in the USA where he published his book in 1943. Twenty-odd years went by before I saw him again in the Burlington Arcade, on his way to buy cigarettes at Sullivan Powell. We had a happy and hilarious reunion and kept in touch until his death in 1972.

Life at Hamworthy was a trifle disorganised. The colonel left to command a brigade soon after we had reassembled, and his successor was not the man to take a firm grip. We had few vehicles other than a hodge-podge of impressed civilian transport and the role of guarding the coast between Branksome Chine and the Sandbanks Hotel, however necessary, was not inspiring. To make matters worse, Andrew Horsbrugh-Porter and I were not on a very good terms after Dunkirk. He had been through fearful strain as a squadron leader; he had lost three of his officers and several NCOs and men and had himself been wounded. Added to which (we were unaware of this at the time), his delightful wife Mary was due to have a baby about the time that we embarked (in fact I think the child was born the day we landed). He had done supremely well, receiving a well-earned DSO, but his nerves were now in a poor state and there was no Herbert Lumsden to control him, nor was there Henry de la Falaise to act as mentor. He had to take it out on someone, and I became the recipient of one or two pieces of sarcasm which I felt unable to accept. Had I been older and less strung up myself and had there been some senior officer of character around, it would all have blown over, but Andrew had such a strong personality that he intimidated the poor little colonel and a very uneasy atmosphere ensued.

There was no proper mess at the time and I had moved into a house called 'Hove To' at Sandbanks which had been taken by the Byasses. 'The most dangerous woman in London' was amazingly capable in organising the comforts of life, not excepting accommodation for various female guests, but she also derived a certain satisfaction from the situation just described and was not averse to stirring the pot.

I have to say that we also had a great deal of fun during this somewhat frenetic period. The very agreeable Sandbanks Hotel, only a few hundred yards from 'Hove To', was under orders to be shut down within a month or two to form part of the coastal defences. Its management seemed anxious that its cellar should be empty before then and the hotel became the scene of almost continuous saturnalia. The band was still playing and there was a very good chef.

One of those who enjoyed its amenities was the chaplain, never averse to social pleasures, who eventually rejoined us after some hair-raising adventures. He reported unfavourably on some senior cleric who had beaten a rapid retreat from France with the words 'God bless you, Macmanaway, look after the lads here. I wish I could be with you, but the Chaplain General has called me home.' It made one think of the padre in Siegfried Sassoon's *Memoirs of an Infantry Officer,* reassuringly accompanying an outgoing draft of troops as far as the station.

Bill Mabbott, whose administrative system was so good that during the campaign we certainly never lacked for supplies, appeared after a time, having been thought to be missing. He had been returning from leave on the *Lancastria,* due to reach Le Havre soon after the start of the fighting, when the ship had been attacked from the air.

It received several direct hits, one down a funnel, and Bill and others were blown into the sea. I have always been told that he and the late Peter Farquhar were the heroes of this disaster, saving numbers of lives and restoring confidence amongst the survivors. It was a relief to have him back. Even if we had no armoured cars and few arms, we knew that we would be adequately clothed and fed.

Eventually we received some very dangerous vehicles called Beaverettes, presumably named in honour of Lord Beaverbrook who then loomed large in national affairs. These were rather fast Standards fitted with a sheet of boiler plate on oak backing as protection in front. Visibility for the driver was bad and the armament was only a Bren gun. But there was nothing else available until the following spring and, acquiring some No. 11 wireless sets, we became mobile and operational again, being sent in July to Suffolk to be handy for the anticipated German invasion.

Before moving there, Tim Morris, one of our best sergeants, and some eight selected troopers were whisked away for unspecified 'Special Duties'. On arrival in London they discovered they were to act as drivers and mobile guards to the King and to the Royal Family and remained in this role until such time as the Household Cavalry could take over its proper and traditional task. They only rejoined us in the late summer of 1942.

'A' Squadron landed up at Long Melford Hall, near Sudbury, but I spent little time there, as even the new colonel thought that Andrew and I were better apart and I became intelligence officer, driving about a wonderfully quiet East Anglia to make contact with LDVs (as the Home Guard was then called), coastguards and local authorities, as well as the neighbouring troops.

Within a few weeks, however, three of us were under orders to go to Ulster to help with the training of the newly revived North Irish Horse, of John Erne was to have taken command. My companions were Maurice Barker, a handsome and intelligent Cambridge graduate who had been one of the six young officers to join us in late 1938, and Gordon Smith, called 'Long Distance' Smith (why I do not know, except to differentiate him from 'British' Smith), who was on the Supplementary Reserve. We made a tedious journey by train to Stranraer in order to take the non-existent boat to Larne but happily 'Long Distance' had contacts with the RAF and we flew over in a Sunderland flying boat to Portrush where the North Irish Horse had their headquarters, astonishing the natives by landing in the harbour. Ulster, I always understood, was not subject to conscription, the belief being that it would provide a continuing stream of volunteers. How true this was to prove later remains a little doubtful, but there were certainly a fair number who came from over the border. In any event the North Irish Horse themselves were not short of local recruits, a large proportion being of officer material.

It was to be an armoured car regiment and as they were all keen to learn everything we could teach them, we had quite a tiring and testing time assisting with their training. Their own officers were very good, though some were a bit long in the tooth, but the War Office had not helped matters by drafting in a few cavalry officers whom neither their own regiments or anyone else wanted. Added to which a disastrous regular commanding officer had been appointed, I presume when John Erne was killed, and though he had been removed just as we arrived, his successor was little better.

Soon after our arrival we had been summoned to the presence of the divisional general, Adrian Carton de Wiart. He received us with great courtesy but then surprised us (we were all subalterns) by saying that he had sacked one commanding officer of the North Irish Horse and was quite prepared to sack another one. He had a wonderful contempt for the War Office, declaring that if he had any more nonsense he was 'going directly to Winston'. He said, quite frankly, that he wanted to know what was happening and relied on us as outside observers. A few days later his delightful elderly ADC, Fitzgerald, an Irish Guardsman, sought me out and announced – with that implicit belief that everyone in Ireland knows everyone else – 'You'll know David Dawnay, well the General is getting him here as second in command and then everything will be all right.' Indeed it became so, as the sitting CO was gently unseated and David, an Irishman, a 10th Hussar and a star polo player, took command, to raise the regiment to a very high standard and to take it abroad eventually to the First Army in North Africa. After he was promoted it also had a fine record in Italy. David was a very good soldier and a natural leader and there could not have been a better choice. The only sad aspect of all this was that later that year the War Office, probably out of spite to Carton de Wiart, decided to arm the North Irish Horse with tanks, so most of our work was wasted. However, they were very grateful to us so maybe some of our schemes and TEWTs had been of benefit. Certainly one of the former had demanded cool heads when owing to a confusion of signals and map reading the best part of a squadron was discovered to be on the wrong side of the border with Eire, which, despite the enormous amount of its young men in British service, was very strictly neutral. Fortunately local frontier relationships were then amicable and after much talk and unbelievable amounts of whiskey, the incident was agreed never to have taken place. The general, who had his own sources of information, inevitably learnt about it and, far from being angry or upset, indicated that we might have pushed on and motored down to Dublin to take over the country. He was a real salamander but had such charm and good manners, combined with a splendid appearance, that it was obvious why troops had followed him into so many forlorn situations.

Thanks to natural local hospitality and the innumerable introductions that had been arranged by our chaplain, not all of them of a sacred nature, we were entertained almost too well at times, but all told it was an agreeable straightforward existence without the emotional or physical disturbances of the last few months. We also felt we were being of assistance to the war effort.

It was towards Christmas when the news came of the impending conversion of the North Irish Horse to tanks, and after prolonged farewells we returned to England where the regiment was now quartered near Reigate, forming the reconnaissance element of the 1st Armoured Division, under the command of Willoughby Norrie. The latter, a much-respected and competent figure, must in the coming months have had his habitual urbanity severely strained by the manner in which his armaments and personnel were removed by higher authority to suit strategic needs elsewhere.

The division consisted originally of the 2nd and 22nd Armoured Brigades, with a support group of Gunners and lorried infantry; but in mid-summer of 1941 the 22nd Armoured Brigade was despatched to Egypt and a little later the 2nd failed to get their promised tanks – also diverted to Egypt – to make good battle losses. The division was not reunited until November, in Libya; by then Willoughby Norrie had been promoted to command 30 Corps in the desert, while Herbert Lumsden, to our joy, became divisional commander under him.

On a rather lower level I was promoted to captain and to the command of Headquarters Squadron, billeted in the village of Charlwood, which now lies practically on the periphery of Gatwick Airport (at that time the area covered by the latter enclosed a steeplechase course and a tiny civilian airfield). But I was quite happy, after a month or two, to go as second in command to William Browne-Clayton at 'B' Squadron, a little further away at Norwood Hill.

The squadron was billeted around the village of Leigh in a then quiet and unspoiled area of Surrey. Our mess lay in a tarted up very partially Tudor house called Little Mynthurst, where I presided over the young gentlemen, as William Browne-Clayton lived out with his wife. He was not the most communicative or imaginative of persons though friendly and good-hearted. He expected me to do quite a lot, which I didn't mind, though sometimes it was difficult to discern his wishes. Luckily John Clark-Kennedy, who had been one of his troop leaders in 1940, was still in the squadron and could more easily interpret the words of the prophet. John was an ideal companion and a tower of strength and both he and I were in despair at the ineptitude of some of the new officers. Eventually, by working on William and a fair amount of intrigue, we improved matters considerably by collecting Matt Abraham and John Stimpson. The former, a delightful, forceful and original personality, was to be an outstanding regimental officer, commanding officer and, later, colonel of the regiment, as well as becoming a distinguished major general. I was rather frightened of him at first, but it was rapidly apparent that he was a born tactician with panache as well as a quick brain. John Stimpson, tall and thin, a farmer from Norfolk, was a man of humour and common sense, qualities much needed in war. He too became an exceptional troop leader – happily in my squadron in the desert. He ended the war as ADC to Oliver Leese in the Far East.

Also attached to us was Adrian Batchelor-Taylor, alumnus of Eton and Balliol and a man of letters, or perhaps one should say belletrist. His erudition lay lightly on him, though he was a stickler for the correct use of English, both oral and written. His charm and gentle wit made his friendship during that troubled spring one of its more happy memories. We used to take companionable walks through a deserted countryside where his disquisitions on Lytton Strachey and his circle enabled me to forget the mundane and selfish difficulties of my own life.

Everyone became devoted to him and his heart was truly with the 12th Lancers although he had been commissioned in the Scots Greys. At the time of our leaving England he joined the 'Phantom' where his intelligence was likely to be well employed, but by means unknown he eventually managed to be transferred to us – though sadly for me, after I had been captured. In Italy he was not only an exceptional troop leader but also carried out, singly, heroic expeditions on foot behind the German positions for which he received a well-deserved MC. Tragically, he was wounded accidentally, becoming paralysed in his legs, a condition to which he adjusted himself with quite admirable stoicism.

There were other diversions while quartered at 'Little Minto', as Adrian called it. I had the use of a nice chestnut horse lent to me by the late Harold Field (about whom I could write a chapter), and was able to hunt, not infrequently, with the Crawley and Horsham, then and for many years to come presided over by Molly Gregson, a lady whose son, Charles, was to join us and become an outstanding officer before being killed in action. Also, I had a few days with the Southdown, little thinking that within fifteen years I would become one of its joint masters.

During our absence in Ulster, various internal convulsions

had been taking place, not all of them for the good. With the expansion of the Army we had to assist in the creation of another armoured car regiment, to be called the 27th Lancers. Originally this was to be commanded by 'British' Smith, but Andrew Horsbrugh-Porter succeeded him after a short time and from the beginning had the dominant say in its formation. Inevitably we had to provide a fair amount of officers and other ranks but it seemed that Andrew had so worked on our colonel that an excessive amount of cream had been skimmed away for the benefit of the new child. With a stronger man at the helm this would have been managed in a more equitable manner to say the least of it, and the loss of good NCOs was particularly galling. Added to which, we ourselves were expanded, as at least one result of the recent campaign was to show that we had been seriously undermanned. Each squadron was increased to five troops so that when fully deployed some fifteen patrols could be provided to cover a much wider front. All this needed more men and more officers. The former appeared and were ready to be moulded into whatever shape was required. Of the latter we had a certain number of very high quality ready to join, but with the remainder the poor colonel and his adjutant had been none too clever. I think it was Dick McCreery who had repeated, before the war, the dictum of Wellington that there were no indifferent soldiers, only indifferent officers.

The atmosphere was gloomy and not helped by an intensely cold winter and prolonged delays in the delivery of new Humber armoured cars. A lot of people had disappeared either temporarily or permanently. Even the parson had been promoted and translated to divisional headquarters, where he developed an invaluable natural faculty for keeping his ear close to the ground. The doctor was still with us and thank God, Bill Mabbott; Rodney Palmer commanded my old squadron, with whom I longed to be back; Rupert Byass had gone to the 27th Lancers, while Dozy Willis was still with 'C' Squadron.

Soon after our return Dozy had announced, to our considerable surprise, that he was about to be married to Hermione Baddeley – an unexpected union, as indeed were so many in wartime. She was the greatest fun and wonderful company, but had little intention of quitting the boards for marital bliss. The young marrieds rented a house near Reigate and Hermione went on tour, while Dozy was left with two teenage stepchildren who gave him a fair amount of trouble. The girl, Pauline, who was immensely attractive and, I think, required by her mother to appear younger than she really was, disappeared to London during an air raid. Poor Dozy was distraught about this, but thanks to the ever-resourceful Ned Mann (his military prowess earned him a DSO as a second lieutenant) she was retrieved apparently undamaged.

From the middle of March I kept a diary until we went abroad again in September. I am not particularly proud of it, but it has proved useful in evoking something of the atmosphere of 1941, and of reviving a failing memory. Personally I had various troubles – emotional, economic, and to do with military frustration – but those spring and summer months were certainly romantic and exciting, with nostalgic memories of a background of air raid warnings and the strains of Tim Clayton's band.

On the financial front, all the extravagant chickens of what Tim Bishop called my 'Grassthorpe' days were coming home to roost. Credit, before and even during the war, was easy for young men who gave the appearance of being well-heeled and I had collected a fine core of debts which neither the ingenuity of an infinitely patient bank manager, Mr Spargo, nor the rather ineffective ministrations of the family solicitor could dissolve. Looking back, I feel that I over-emphasised the gravity of the situation, but this was probably an excuse for my lack of moral courage in failing to present my grandmother with my problems. I am sure that with her usual generosity she would have come to my rescue.

Re-reading my diary, with its endless moans about finance, I detect precious little sign of an inhibited style of life. I was still able to hunt intermittently, and I can recall no effort on my part to curtail frequent and expensive dinners at the Mirabelle, nights at the Four Hundred (that roseate haunt of much wartime romance) and considerable sociable drinking at the Ritz Bar. Neil Speke, Tim Bishop and I had some arrangement whereby we could always have rooms in Stanmore Court, in St. James's Street, and we were all members of Boodle's Club. If our pleasures were confined to a small area of the bombed metropolis, they were by no means inexpensive; nor were the taxis that, in times of stress, we were obliged to hire to take us back to our billets. Wartime London did have a very special charm and its atmosphere, if not parochial, was certainly intimate. There were still some parties, women contrived to look glamorous despite the 'austerity' signalised by clothing coupons, and the foreign uniforms of exiled armies added a Continental chic. One seemed to see friends everywhere and it would have been difficult to be lonely. And the Americans had not yet arrived.

When I went abroad again in September a sort of committee was left to handle my finances and by the time I returned to England in 1945 I was once again solvent, if not affluent. To give some idea of the value of money then, I am sure I did not take out with me to the Middle East more than three or four hundred pounds. A captain's pay was around £1 a day or maybe less, and when one became a major it rose to the dizzy sum of twenty-eight shillings. Admittedly, for the year or two I was there I was more in the desert than not, but I cannot recall being overly strapped for cash or thinking of economising when in Cairo or elsewhere.

Military frustration was increased within the regiment at the non-appearance of the promised new armoured cars, the difficulties of training with mocked up vehicles and the somewhat unhappy atmosphere to which I have alluded. Nationally, 1941 was not a glorious year and there was a long way to go until the time following Alamein when Winston Churchill would speak of the 'end of the beginning'. There were endless schemes, endless administrative pinpricks and endless discussions about hypothetical, tactical, strategic and diplomatic situations.

I can say in all honesty that I was glad when we were told in August that our division was going overseas. The thought of having to remain in England for nearly three years until the Normandy invasion is one that sometimes enters my bad dreams. I should probably have ended up in close arrest, or in Broadmoor, or in the divorce court, or even all three. Those of the armed forces who stuck out the long period of waiting and anticipation before seeing action – in most cases for the first time and, in some cases, for the last – deserve all praise for their endurance. Even when I was later a prisoner of war, I received letters from friends at home, in 1943 and 1944, in which it was possible, reading between the lines, to sense the continual ennui that this waiting engendered. I am thankful I had been able to participate in some genuine activity, even if it led to my personal withdrawal from the scene.

One has, and had, much else for which to be grateful, but I have always counted it a blessing that neither my regiment nor I had to be enclosed in tanks. The role of armoured cars, especially in highly mobile warfare, was emphatically that of the old cavalry screen. It was seldom static, always interesting in that one had a wide picture of events, and it was not too dangerous provided one kept one's wits about one. Armoured (tank) regiments did not have a cushy time. They had to face invariable casualties, unpleasant wounds and confined operations, often conducted within that tactical cocoon 'the fog of war' The crews needed great qualities of stamina and courage and one can well understand how the survivors of several engagements tended to become battle weary.

While in Surrey we were subjected to a fairly continuous stream of visitors, presumably sent by the War Office to our division, in which we ourselves seemed to form the point of no return. Some of them stayed, especially two agreeable Canadians from the Manitoba Dragoons. It was not always easy to keep these birds of passage interested or employed and we had a particularly difficult time with a posse of Polish officers, who made heavy inroads into our diminishing supplies of alcohol. Some early Americans, however, the first of their nation we had seen (it was still a while before Pearl Harbour), were highly professional officers. They seemed in no doubt that sooner or later they would be in the war and were anxious to imbibe information. Bill Mabbott, inevitably, served them up a wealth of administrative lore.

During the early months of the year there were some complicated anti-invasion schemes, during which we acted as umpires and radio links, having few vehicles of our own. I have a vivid recollection of conveying an unpalatable message to 'Boy' Browning, then commanding an Independent Guards brigade in the region of Hastings. He subjected me to the most appalling abuse which Adrian Batchelor-Taylor assured me I was lucky to receive, pointing out that in classical times the bearer of bad news would have been slaughtered.

I think it was on the same outing that an elderly senior officer, also an umpire, to whom I reported in the evening, said that he had to go and see if his driver was comfortable – the driver eventually appearing as an immensely pretty girl in the ATS. Perhaps there was a measure of jealousy in my diary note that the British army was becoming *'un bordel ambulant'*.

The spring seemed to go on interminably, only relieved by an expedition of a few days to, of all places, Southport in Lancashire, where four of us were despatched to learn about the intricacies of military pay. In fact it was a refreshing interlude as we were accommodated in an admirable boarding house, with very superior food, walked on the seafront and went to a different music hall every evening. I doubt we learned much of army finance, but it was a welcome escape from the Surrey billets. I was also able to bore my companions sick by reiterating the information that Michael Arlen had written *The Green Hat* in Southport in order to find a milieu unconnected with the sophistication of Mayfair. I very much admired Arlen in those days – he was one of the habitués of the Ritz Bar.

We were entrusted with a staff car and drove back across the heart of England. I noted in my diary how quiet the country was: apart from military and RAF traffic on the main roads and some aircraft in the sky, the inner villages and countryside were as silent as the grave.

On my return to Norwood Hill, I went to London, following a major air raid which had taken place on the night of 16 April. I recorded the following account:

I went to London after an early lunch today, only for the afternoon, in view of last night's activities. Trains rather deranged, and I did not get to the dentist until after three, he found one tooth far too old and collapsed to mend, so pulled it out, which was rather a bore. However, for once in my life I had time to get a few things done. London appeared as if Nero was still fiddling. The little I saw was all rather messed up, especially around Jermyn Street, which was railed off, and fires were still raging; St James's Street a mass of pumps, hoses and AFS men all looking completely beat. Thousands of people were walking about through a sea of glass and debris, enjoying the sights and breathing in the smoke and dust-charged air. I think the Conservative Club is the only one usable in St James's Street. Everyone was expecting another appalling blitz, but there was only one rather sterile alert. I ran into Rupert and realised that, possibly, I might not return from London as early as I intended. We went to see Fred Astaire's new picture, a relaxation with Miss Goddard so attractive. We walked from the cinema to the Mirabelle. It was dark and very warm and the air was full of dust. Dimly, one saw vague figures flitting about amongst the craters and piles of rubbish. It was most reminiscent of coming into some Belgium or French town last May in the evening and trying to determine whether the shadows were German tanks or merely the wagons of refugees. As always, it is the smell that brings back half-forgotten pictures quicker than anything else.

At the beginning of May we moved to a tented camp, Tidworth Pennings, 'beneath the endless patter of raindrops and the strain of a communal life nourished by Shaw Porter' (a local and rapacious caterer), remaining there until within a few weeks of embarking for the Middle East. Although the diary contains the usual complaints and moans, I do not think life there was too unpleasant. On the whole the weather was good, Salisbury Plain was quite a healthy place and we at last started to get some armoured cars that were a significant improvement on the poor old Morrises that we had abandoned in France. There was great enthusiasm at this time for motor-cycle combinations and we experimented endlessly employing a mixture of these and scout cars with the armoured cars, although once in the desert we reverted to the original troop of three armoured cars as the basic unit. I think this formation was unaltered until later in the war, especially in Italy where different tactics required different patterns of vehicles.

Alcohol was supposedly in short supply, though considering the regimental consumption this must have been a relative term. I think I was responsible for augmenting our stocks and cannot have done too badly as various entries record the location of 'five dozen Ruinart 1928 and a case of Kummel', 'four dozen more Montrachet' (it can't have been Le Montrachet?) and so on. Another interesting contemporary note is about seeing a beautiful girl buying lemons in a shop in Amesbury. Lemons at this time were as common as the four-leaf clover. Beautiful girls were more in evidence, but we did manage to get our lemons and ask the dazzling Debo Cavendish (with her husband) to a party – presumably enlivened by something more than lemonade.

In early July it was announced that Wavell had been sacked and replaced by Auchinleck and very soon after this a probably apocryphal story related that Winston Churchill threw the Military Secretary's Department into dismay by demanding particulars of the life and service of 'General Affleck', choosing to believe that the name was pronounced in the manner of Lord Auchinleck, the father of James Boswell.

Towards the end of the month, the 25th, the Prime Minister himself came down to Tidworth to address the officers of the 1st Armoured Division and to explain why the armoured brigades had again been deprived of their tanks.

Today was the long expected visit of the Prime Minister, the anticipation of which seems to have caused such havoc to people's nerves here. John Wormald [adjutant] seemed on the verge of a nervous breakdown and excelled himself yesterday as he succeeded in producing half the officers in battledress and half in the other kind for the parade. William and I took advantage of the muddle and dressed as gentlemen. Willoughby Norrie came to lunch, even his usual imperturbability seemed a trifle disturbed and he ate very little. Most of the officers in the First Armoured Division were arranged in a fairly cohesive formation in the tattoo area facing the stands. Dotted about were some of the few remaining vehicles, chiefly our armoured cars. As in all performances of this kind everyone had been made to appear far too early so that there was a long wait in the hot sun.

At last there was a vague confusion on our right and one could dimly see cars arriving and people saluting madly and incessantly. A small round figure in light summer grey shot ahead of its entourage and darted amongst a thicket of armoured cars, whence it emerged with Geoff, our Colonel, both moving very fast. We could see them looking at a new Daimler that had just arrived and everyone became frozen while the cameras did their work. The cortège now drew nearer across our right front where it again stopped to be introduced to some of the staff. Finally it came fully into sight. Winston, Willoughby, Alan Brooke, a gaggle of ill-dressed and evil-looking generals, some obvious Americans, one of them Harriman, a neat little naval officer and two or three elderly decayed gentlemen – the eldest wore a boater – who seemed to have been precipitated into all this from the moribund gloom of the Athenaeum.

He seemed very tired and pale and spoke in a very small voice, despite microphones. Really, he had disappointingly little to say, except how unfortunate it was that we had to keep losing our tanks, but that production was infinitely better thanks to Mr Harriman, etc., etc., and that soon it would be possible to equip one complete armoured division every few weeks. We must watch out after the first of September as an invasion was again very likely. Rather an anticlimax as we were all prepared for fire and brimstone.

He then walked around the ranks a bit, he stopped and talked for a minute to that prosy old Jubie Lancaster* who commands a battalion in the Support Group, and finally climbed into an immense black Rolls-Royce with Alan Brooke and disappeared with our cheers and with all his advisers, pressmen and whatnot in a fleet of staff cars behind. So it ended. Rodney's brother, who came to dinner and who is an MP and whom I dislike, said Winston is very worried over the statement he has to make on production and is unapproachable.

In early August we received information that we would be going abroad in September. At the same time it became apparent that the colonel was being superseded, ostensibly for health reasons. His successor was Peter Burne, virtually unknown to most of his officers, as he had been away with the French Army for three or four years. Intelligent and a very good linguist, he was not always easy and inspired no great affection. His second in command, Sam Strang, whom we also had not seen for some years, was a laid-back New Zealander, of little competence but full of endearing traits. Of the regiment which was to go abroad, Rodney Palmer was to continue commanding 'A' Squadron, William Browne-Clayton 'B' with me as his second in command, but poor old Dozy Willis had been found unfit and was in a terrible state having to remain in England. I think, too, that the theatrical marriage was by this time not going too well. Maurice Barker was to command 'C' Squadron temporarily until we arrived in Egypt (it was now agreed tacitly that this

*Colonel C.G. Lancaster was a Conservative MP for Fylde in Lancashire for some twenty years. On this warm occasion he had brought all his Sherwood Forester officers fully accoutred for war – steel helmets, gas masks, entrenching tools, compasses and other paraphernalia. They were all hot and uncomfortable. One of the divisional staff reported that when Winston spied the gallant colonel he greeted him with these words. 'Ah, Lancāster, itching, I observe, to get at the foe!' I do not think he came with us to the Middle East.

might be our destination) where Arthur Gemmell, who was already there, would take it over.

Towards the end of September it fell to my lot to take all the armoured cars up to Birkenhead for embarkation. We took no lorries, or 'B' vehicles as they were called, as these were to be provided when we reached the Middle East. This was an agreeable expedition which went off well, and at the end of our labours, before returning by train the next day, those officers who were with me spent a somewhat riotous and valedictory night in the Adelphi Hotel, Liverpool. While there, I was told on the telephone by the adjutant that I had been offered a squadron in the 27th Lancers by Andrew Horsbrugh-Porter. I asked him to decline on my behalf.

The next day we drifted back to Wiltshire by a dilatory military train, which I hoped would arrive at Westbury not too late, as a party was being given that night by Daphne Weymouth, whose beauty and hospitality did so much to enliven the wartime scene, and who is so well recalled by Conrad Russell. I eventually arrived in a deserted mess, to be greeted with written messages to 'come on as soon as possible', but while eating a cold and unpalatable supper I was summoned to the telephone personally by Andrew Horsbrugh-Porter calling from Yorkshire. It was to emphasise that he wanted me to come to him as a squadron leader and not to go with the regiment to the Middle East. At first I thought he was joking but the tone of his voice soon dispelled the idea. In vain I told him that my bags were packed, my affairs settled up, my fond farewells made and so on. He took my refusal badly – 'Just the sort of bloody-minded way I should expect you to behave, missing the chance of a lifetime.' We parted coolly and I don't remember any good wishes bestowed upon me. The telephone call gave me no taste for festivities and I retired gloomily to bed, where I stayed despite my kind friends coming to get me up.

As it turned, out the 27th Lancers did not go abroad until some time in 1944. The interval of waiting must have been extremely trying. Andrew commanded them in Italy with distinction, winning a bar to his DSO. When I emerged from prison in the spring of 1945 plans were in hand for the running down of the 27th. Some of its personnel were to be transferred to the mother regiment of which Andrew was to be the commanding officer. Once again I received peremptory messages demanding my return, but – apart from personal reasons – I thought I was by then quite unfitted for soldiering and was only anxious to leave the Army.

At some time in 1945 I was dining in London with my future wife and he walked into the restaurant. She always maintains that I immediately vanished through the kitchen, showing presence of mind but little bravery. When he retired some years later, he took on various sporting literary jobs with certain journals, with a long stint as hunting correspondent of *The Field*. With his usual courage he was prepared to ride strange horses in strange countries and his accounts, those of a modern Pomponius Ego, were well put together and read very well. Eventually, we were on terms of amity and he came to stay at home on two or three occasions when I was Master of Hounds, but I was inclined to steer his conversation towards sporting rather than military reminiscence. Sometimes the mention of a name or place from the war would make him show the white of his eyes. It was a relief that all rancour had gone before he died.

Re-Encounter

VOYAGE

It was dark, wet and very early in the morning when on 29 September I marched through the empty streets of Westbury at the rear of 'B' Squadron on the way to the station. I chiefly remember my anxiety about various items of my kit and the hope that the business of embarkation would permit a little well-earned rest in the afternoon; all highly material and vastly different from the welter of excitement in which I sailed to France in 1939. Perhaps there can be only one '*partant pour la Syrie*' in a lifetime.

At the station, as the men were hustled briskly into the train, I found myself hanging about the platform, condoling with those of my brother officers who were suffering from alcoholic remorse. Smallridge arrived to say that my belongings were on board. He, too, looked rather unwell. Then we were all told to get in and a moment later the train steamed out of Westbury - only to stop within a few hundred yards as though for second thoughts. Those of us familiar with the vagaries of military travel dozed uncomfortably in our carriage and I only properly awoke when we had pulled into Avonmouth alongside a grey and rather dreary-looking ship. The whole regiment bundled out and occupied itself with enormous supplies of tea and sandwiches served in a large shed – administrative foresight that turned to double vision when, after embarking with unexpected ease, we found an even bigger meal awaiting us on board. By midday I had mounted the gangway and quit the soil of England for an unspecified number of years.

Under her drab exterior the *Highland Brigade* was remarkably spacious though it seemed that the men were going to be rather tightly packed. There was temporarily bitter confusion between decks, with a mass of milling soldiers trying to stow their kit and overcome their surprise at the hammocks in which they were to sleep for the next six weeks. However, with the help of a few sailors order of a sort was established and Neil and I went off to find our own quarters.

On the way we met the captain, who with a smack of the eighteenth century introduced himself as 'master'. We later discovered that he had commanded a destroyer in the First World War – a long row of ribbons pointed to some service of distinction. He greeted us warmly and personally found our cabins for us. In appearance rather like a rural Pickwick, Captain Cox was a rare mixture of charm and efficiency. He treated everyone as if they were delightful naughty children and his management of the ship was reflected in the good nature of his hard-working crew. Both he and they did everything they could for our comfort and well-being, and we were all profoundly sorry to leave the *Highland Brigade* when we reached Durban. The Merchant Navy receives very little ungrudging praise, but I can vouch for the gratitude of some six hundred men.

There were four officers to a cabin. Although I remember commenting on this as unnecessarily excessive (little knowing that within eighteen months I should be living in a small room cheek by jowl with seventeen other people), we were really comfortable, with the advantage that the cabin that I shared with three of the 'B' Squadron subalterns was an outside one.

All the military personnel were nominally under the command of a desiccated and sardonic veteran called Colonel Gale who was assisted by a very tiresome adjutant, whom I remember chiefly for a Glaswegian accent and an ability to sweat freely under all conditions. In equatorial waters he prudently augmented his dress with a towel thrust negligently into his bosom. The couple were not highly popular with Captain Cox whose authority they were inclined to usurp.

He countered this very successfully by dealing direct with Peter Burne and the CO of the RASC (our fellow passengers) and paying little attention to the others' bleating requests for recognition. There after Colonel Gale became little more than a figurehead and his only moments of power were during boat drills when he majestically inspected the ship, intermittently blowing a whistle, with the adjutant in attendance bearing a file of quite irrelevant papers.

The legitimate business of the *Highland Brigade,* in the intervals of conveying troops to the Middle East, was the South American meat trade. Consequently she was uncommonly well victualled and we all fed and drank (troopships only became dry after the United States entered the war) to perfection throughout the voyage. The men's food alone would have done credit to any London club.

The day after leaving Avonmouth we were joined by a light cruiser which escorted us up St George's Channel to the Clyde. Here we joined the rest of the convoy, which contained most of the 1st Armoured Division. A surprising number of people had already become rather queasy at the motion of the ship and were taken in hand by Charles Morrison-Bell, who for some reason knew about sea sickness from working in the management of the Mayfair Hotel. Then, a few days later, we set out into the Atlantic in a great concourse of ships, protected by a formidable escort, including an aircraft carrier. The last sight of Great Britain was a mist-hung cliff which the geographically knowledgeable said was 'Skye or one of those places'.

The voyage was really agreeable and not enlivened by any startling naval incidents, though on two or three occasions we made some very sharp 'jinks', allegedly on account of U-boat alarms, although the crew claimed to know no more than we did. We used to start the day with some fairly gentle PT, followed, when it was warmer, by a bathe. During the morning there were various classes and lectures for the men and we were fairly busy until luncheon. In the afternoon there was boxing or some kind of sport, which had to be watched, but more often there were extra boat drills for the gratification of Colonel Gale. After this one was always free. I found ample leisure to read and so, having provided myself with a tea chest of books, I was perfectly content. There was always the sea and the ever-changing movements of the convoy to watch and, of course, endless light-hearted gossip and inaccurate prognostication about the future. There was even an excellent, if sometimes rather overpowering, RASC band.

In England the regiment had always been split up into widely separated squadrons and one now had a chance of talking to new officers and men who were practically strangers. The ship's company were always ready to while away half an hour or so if they were not busy, and some of them had had the most remarkable lives. There was a bath steward called Killick who always breakfasted in one of his bathrooms off a bottle of Guinness. He had started his career as a valet to some noblemen in whose service I fancy he had come to grief, and thereafter had drifted round the world in a variety of employment – mainly disreputable. I envied him a lot of his beachcombing life; he had derived much enjoyment from it besides developing a most admirable philosophy. Along with several others of the crew he turned out to be unexpectedly well-read.

Then there was the chief steward who had been 'twenty-five years on the fever coast'. Where this was none of us was quite certain but his assurance forbade any ignorant inquiry. He was a subtle flatterer and his remarks of 'Lord, what strong heads you gentlemen have' and 'The wine steward was only saying to me this morning, sir, that he'd never seen men keep it up so and look so well' were not without their effect, as the ship was dry of all but hard liqour (she carried a seemingly inexhaustible supply) when we reached Durban.

After three or four weeks we made the west coast of Africa and put into Freetown for a few days to take on fresh water.

It was appallingly hot, without any breath of breeze. A few people went ashore to visit the dentist and returned with the most alarming tales of everyone being limp and spineless with the humid heat of the place. Michael de Piro had a brother there, in the Gunners, who came to see him. He looked very thin and washed out and said that Freetown was deadly dull and had the atmosphere of a third-rate Turkish bath.

It was the beginning of November, in the evening, when Table Mountain suddenly appeared out of the darkening distance and one half of the convoy turned into Cape Town while our part continued to Durban. General speculation during the voyage had envisaged Durban as a kind of marine Klondike which would obviously be 'pretty impossible', but from the sea the city looked clean, modern and generally enchanting, and so it proved to be.

We were due on arrival to carry out the most complicated administrative manoeuvres, the thought of which made my heart sink. On such occasions the second in command of a squadron had to carry a mass of facts and figures in his head. What we actually had to do was to leave the *Highland Brigade,* go to a transit camp, stay there a few days and then re-embark on a Dutch liner called the *Nieuw Amsterdam*. All this was duly accomplished but a tragedy occurred at the outset against which any temporary difficulties could seem no more than petty inconvenience.

The afternoon that we berthed all ranks were allowed on shore but had to return by 2 a.m. Tim, Neil and I went off together, and after wandering agape about the city, found ourselves in the Durban Club where we were handsomely entertained. Somehow or other we came to meet a Mrs Leary, who insisted on taking us to her house and extended us the most lavish hospitality, introducing us to her family and everyone else in sight. They all seemed inordinately pleased to see us, notwithstanding the fact that countless convoys had preceded ours and might have tarnished the gilt on the gingerbread. If they had, no one in Durban said anything about it and I preserve the most grateful memories of the universal kindness.

It was a hilarious evening. Sometime after midnight we found ourselves in what I thought was a very attractive nightclub – though at that stage one was viewing the scene through rose-coloured spectacles. To our amusement the perspiring ship's adjutant, Captain Tate, still armed with his towel, was consoling himself in a dark corner with a lady of Brobdingnagian proportions. With the greatest reluctance, as we saw the clock approaching 2 a.m., we left the scene of giddy joy to others who were not apparently bound by the same restriction.

The ship was very quiet when we returned. We went foraging for some beer and sandwiches – there was a night watchman in the bowels of the ship whose acquaintance we had previously made and who could provide these things. On emerging onto the cabin deck again we encountered our doctor who said there had been a most frightful accident. Maurice Barker had fallen over the side and got caught up in some ropes. 'They're bringing him up on deck. Come and give a hand.'

Smallridge arrived to supplement this story, having been over the side and almost into the water in his efforts to help. We went up on deck and found Maurice lying in the middle of a little group, two of whom were giving him artificial respiration. We all worked on this in turns and at one time it seemed that he gave signs of returning consciousness. After a time, however, it was apparent to both doctors – the ship's doctor was there as well – that life was extinct and Maurice's body was carried away to the hospital. The full horror took a while to sink in. We were all physically exhausted, and Peter Burne wisely sent us straight off to bed before we started talking.

I slept an hour or two but then awoke and went out on deck to a wonderfully fragrant dawn. Presently one or two of the others appeared. It was difficult to speak of the business but gradually we pieced together what had happened. Maurice had returned with some companions a short time before us and gone on his own to get some fresh air on the boat deck. There were no railings between the boats, and standing on the side away from the quay he must have lost his balance and fallen over. This would not have mattered if he had fallen clear, as the splash of his entering the water would have been heard by the watch and the sentries. Unfortunately he became entangled in some of the ropes hanging down the ship's side and, in struggling to get free, he brought all the pressure onto his neck. By the time assistance arrived he was hanged.

It was a ghastly affair. He was my exact contemporary and I had known him very well indeed since he joined the regiment from Cambridge in 1938. He was a person of singular charm, though to a few people he had a manner which gave an appearance of conceit. Nothing could have been further from the truth; he had, rather, a certain deprecating shyness, which to his friends was very attractive. He was a fine sportsman with a deep love of the country and was no mean ornithologist. His consuming interest in birds had taken him to some outlandish places and he was singularly well travelled for his age. In the French campaign he had been regimental transport officer and, owing to the wide distances we covered, had had to compete with almost impossible difficulties of supply. It was largely thanks to him that we never lacked petrol and rations. He looked at life with a very original slant and his companionship was always refreshing as he was a shrewd judge of character without being in the least cynical. It was only in the weeks following his death that I came to realise how very much we missed him.

All this cast a blight over the rest of the time in Durban and though hospitality and kindness remained undiminished, no one had much zest to enjoy them. We stayed a few days in a very well run transit camp at Clairwood Race Course and then went on board the *Nieuw Amsterdam*. This was an enormous Dutch luxury liner, completed only just before the war. Into her had been packed some 5,000 troops, chiefly South African, with the eternal Gale in command. For him the *Nieuw Amsterdam* was a very much tougher proposition than the *Highland Brigade* and, as we were the only people he knew, he called upon us to carry out the police duties. These were very strenuous, as the South Africans were disinclined for any form of discipline. The food and accommodation compared rather ill with the other ship and the prevailing impression was that the Dutch crew were performing their duties very much under compulsion, though we could not help but feel sorry for them, with their country under German occupation and with no hope of being reunited with their families until after the war. Their officers were very smart and efficient though one saw little of them.

HMS *Repulse* escorted us as far as Aden. By way of farewell she 'manned ship' and steamed at speed past us with her entire crew cheering. She then made the curt and businesslike signal of 'Soldiers, fight well and good luck', and disappeared over the horizon. Within a matter of weeks, she and the *Prince of Wales* had been sunk with most of their crews when they were destroyed by Japanese aircraft in Far Eastern waters.

At Aden we left the convoy and travelled alone up the Red Sea, very rapidly, which had the merit of keeping the ship cool. After Maurice's death I had been given command of 'C' Squadron, and was very busy throughout the short voyage getting to know the men and discussing desert tactics, about which most of us knew extraordinarily little. Edward Mann was my second in command and as he was a close personal friend, besides being a most reliable officer, I could not have been more content. All the subalterns and most of the senior NCOs I already knew as I had started my service in 'C' Squadron five years before. Delighted though I was to have the squadron, I was fairly certain that it would not be for long. Arthur Gemmell, who was years senior to me, was in Egypt and anxious to return to the regiment. He also had the considerable benefit of desert experience. I composed myself philosophically to await the future.

When we reached Suez the first people to come on board were Herbert Lumsden and Arthur, and I realised that my crowns would have to go into retreat. Herbert looked his usual immaculate self and was pleased to see us though I think we were even more pleased to learn he had flown out from England to take command of our division. He reckoned that we would be sent up to the desert as soon as our vehicles were unloaded, as there was a constant demand for armoured car regiments.

Peter Burne was very nice to me about the squadron and said that he would promote me again at the earliest opportunity and that meanwhile he would like me to be his liaison officer. This I jumped at, as I was secretly dreading a return to being a second in command. The new job would be very interesting and also, what I valued more, very independent.

DESERT NOVITIATE

Less than a fortnight later two Ford utility cars were speeding along the coast road to the Western Desert. The leading one contained the colonel and his intelligence officer, Gerald Churchill, a servant and a driver, and was beautifully fitted up for a long campaign. The other car was driven by an obtuse Yorkshireman called Hassall, and was full of a heterogeneous confusion of equipment, myself and Smallridge. The HQ sergeant-major had been very solicitous over my safety, and had provided me with a Bren gun, in a box, which took up an enormous amount of room. Subsequently I returned it to him, saying that the discomforts of the journey had been such that I would make do in the desert with my revolver.

The previous ten days had been very busy for everyone and I had spent my time pursuing recalcitrant supplies over the length of Egypt. After landing at Suez, we had entrained for Abbassia, on the outskirts of Cairo, which was the base for most of the armoured elements. We got in very late at night and as I stepped onto the platform the first person I saw was my friend George Murray-Smith, just arrived with some of the 7th Hussars, who had had a very rough time at the Battle of Sidi Rezegh. We arranged to meet on the morrow but I was sent off elsewhere and never saw him again until after the war, in which he had the distinction of collecting three MCs.

The colonel had preceded the regiment by two or three days, going ahead to GHQ 8th Army at Fort Maddalena, where we were to join him. We started in the dawn.

The road stretched on for miles. On the right was a dull blue Mediterranean and on the left an endlesss expanse of almost flat desert, chiefly scrub and gravel, empty save for an occasional herd of wild camels. The monotony became rather overpowering and I slept until we reached Mersa Matruh. Here we left the coast road and after eating our lunch started driving on a compass bearing for Maddalena. This was something quite new to Gerald and me (in practice, at any rate) and we assimilated as best we could the colonel's expert instructions. The going was smooth, mostly level ground, and it was very exhilarating driving fast towards the horizon, sitting up on top of the car, compass in hand. We broke our journey that night at some dry well, or *bir,* and reached Maddalena the following evening. It seemed rather miraculous arriving at the right destination when there was the whole of Libya in which to get lost.

Army HQ was a collection of camouflaged vehicles and tents all festooned with wireless aerials and telephone wires. The whole lay under a permanent pall of dust raised from an adjacent airfield. We were very hospitably entertained to dinner in one of the messes, and I was rather surprised at the excellent meal, as I had imagined everyone living on bully beef and biscuit.

We spent a day or two here, with the colonel visiting the big shots while we gossiped diffidently with the lesser fry, trying to learn a little without too obviously betraying our ignorance. Some of the slang in current use was perplexing. 'Swanning', we discovered, meant wandering aimlessly about the desert without any apparent motive – an occupation in which even the most hardened veterans were apt to indulge. There was also a lot of talk about 'Honeys' and it was some time before we found out that these were the American-made General Stuart light tanks.

As soon as the regiment arrived, a trifle dazed by its first desert trip, we were sent on to 30 Corps, commanded by Willoughby Norrie. This formation, principally engaged in investing Bardia and the Halfaya Pass, had little use for armoured cars, and we were accordingly despatched to 13 Corps (Lieutenant-General Godwin-Austen), which after relieving Tobruk was now operating against the mobile Axis forces. The 7th Armoured Division, to which we were finally sent, was in this corps. I started on a series of long solitary trips to their different headquarters, and fairly soon found myself confident with a compass, so that I could rely on arriving roughly where I wanted. Smallridge turned himself into a more than adequate cook and within a week we had completely adapted ourselves to a nomadic existence.

13 Corps headquarters were rather elusive, and I was unable to reach them on the evening I intended. It was one of Libya's rare rainy nights and I counted myself lucky in finding the shelter of a recently vacated Italian fort at Acroma. Unfortunately the place was infested with vermin.

The 7th Armoured Division had an immensely high reputation. It was commanded by General Gott, a more than able soldier with a delightful personality, invariably referred to as 'Strafer'. He was later killed in the air shortly after being appointed army commander. In the division was the 7th

Support Group which under Jock Campbell, a heroic figure in the Carton de Wiart tradition, had developed a style of warfare all its own for the very effective harassing of the Germans. At the more critical times of the campaign, when all our armour was exhausted, it often happened that the Support Group and a couple of armoured car regiments were all that faced the enemy, and they always contrived both to worry him considerably and to give an impression of greater strength. The 11th Hussars, our opposite regiment, of whom we had heard nothing but the highest praise, were also in this formation. We were a little anxious over our lack of knowledge of the desert and rather overconscious of appearing tyros to them, but everyone was most considerate and we were guided on our way with helpful advice and assistance.

From now on (early December 1941) until the middle of January, 13 Corps pursued Rommel's forces which were withdrawing in good order across the desert to the bottleneck beyond Agheila. Though reinforced by 22nd Armoured Brigade (Brigadier Scott-Cockburn) it possessed little striking force and could only harass the enemy. We gradually became used to our own work of reconnaissance and observation, and troop leaders began to have some knowledge of what enemy vehicles looked like at a distance, and of how to identify them. Our supply problem, too, eased itself, and within a week or two the rather complicated system of replenishment was working very smoothly.

I had plenty to do and was perpetually on the move between RHQ and different headquarters. The desert, despite a first appearance of monotony, had really a surprising variety of contour and scenery. For all its aridity some life flourished there, and one seldom travelled a long distance without seeing wild camels, gazelle or a pack of sand grouse. In warmer weather iguanas and scorpions and other rather uninviting reptiles appeared out of holes in the ground. Sometimes one met an odd Arab trekking serenely along with a couple of heavily laden donkeys, and one day, when I was driving with Peter Burne in some quite hilly country, we saw a golden eagle.

At that time of year it was very cold at night, with a heavy dew. The days were by no means warm and one always needed two or three sweaters. Everyone was wonderfully well, living constantly in the open air on a rather spare diet. In such physical circumstances one's outlook changed and one felt, despite the immediate responsibilities, agreeably detached and free of the more tiresome trammels of the world. Perhaps, in my case, too much so, as I recollect being severely admonished and urged to take the war more seriously and in a less dilettante manner.

While the regiment was operating on the southern flank of the division, Rodney Palmer's squadron ('A') was pushed on very fast to Fort M'sus, still supposed to be in the hands of the Italians, with a view to rounding them up. After the squadron had left, some aerial photographs of the place arrived at RHQ and with these I was sent off in pursuit. M'sus was forty or fifty miles away, but after completing the distance I could see no signs of a fort or of the squadron, and began to think that I had made a grave error in navigation. After searching the horizon vainly with my glasses, I eventually spotted a troop of armoured cars, which I pursued and found to belong to Rodney, to whom I was directed. They had had the same trouble finding their destination, and our *amour propre* was not fully salved until we were told by Jock Campbell that in this area there was a discrepancy on the map of six or seven miles.

Fort M'sus, which lay on the side of a considerable wadi, might well have formed the background of one of P. C. Wren's stories. The Italians had only quitted it an hour or two before 'A' Squadron arrived, and had evidently made a very hurried departure. In the kitchen the dough for the day's baking was still soft and the cook appeared to have taken nothing with him save his art. There was quite a lot of legitimate loot to be had, of which by far the most welcome was a large supply of excellent bottled mineral water called San Pellegrino. I also managed to acquire a most illuminating collection of anti-British postcards.

While I was talking to Rodney at his HQ in the wadi we were visited, very suddenly, by a German fighter who gave us a rigorous ground strafing, then turned and repeated the process. This went on for some time, as far as I could judge from underneath our armoured car. The pilot unimaginatively failed to vary his line of approach and our Bren gunners began to return his fire with some accuracy. After his fifth or sixth traverse of the valley his engine faltered, and he was forced to 'pancake' two or three miles away, to be gleefully picked up by John Stimpson, the signals officer. But it was a bad period for armoured cars from the air, as 'C' Squadron had a severe bombing attack and rather a lot of casualties and the same day the commanding officer of the Royals, Reggie Heyworth, was killed in this manner.

Within a week or two we were working with 22nd Armoured Brigade in the area of Agedabia-Saunnu, and we took part in a very complex armoured battle at Chor Es Sufan, which followed a sortie in force by the German tanks. I was at brigade HQ most of the time and at one moment we became surrounded and received the full force of the enemy guns, though without any appreciable damage. We were caught in a flat saucer with the enemy on all the commanding ridges, but Brigadier Scott-Cockburn managed to remove his HQ with skill and dexterity. The regiment was watching the flanks of the battle and was to be very active. The colonel was in touch with me on the wireless and kept asking if I saw any signs of our transport echelon which was due to make a rather inopportune arrival. Eventually the entire brigade transport, all 'soft' vehicles, appeared on the horizon and received a bad pounding. They all veered away like a flock of frightened sheep and split up into small groups. Even so the Germans managed to capture some, including two or three of our own lorries and two invaluable squadron quartermaster-sergeants. It was very galling to watch knowing that one could do nothing about it.

This inconclusive battle finally led to a further German withdrawal, and we pushed on through the pass at Sceledima, some troops getting within sight of the sea. It was while going up to one of the squadrons in the early morning that I was nearly captured when I ran straight into four German armoured cars in a hollow. There had obviously been a breakdown, as the men were transferring the equipment of the abandoned vehicle onto the other three. The single sentry was looking in the opposite direction, and I had turned and was well out of range before they loosed off a machine gun. It sounds quite a mild adventure on paper but it was no sort of experience to have before breakfast.

This following up continued for a week or two, with the regiment either under command of 7th Support Group or 22nd Guards Brigade (Brigadier John Marriott), and though we were in contact with the enemy fairly constantly, nothing of much excitement occurred. By the first week of January we were established on a patrol line south-west of Agheila with every prospect of a static period. There was some regrouping and 7th Armoured Division was relieved by the 1st (our own), temporarily commanded by Major-General Messervy as Herbert Lumsden had been wounded by a bomb splinter.

There was little for me to do and the colonel decided to send me back to Tobruk, or further, to try and buy some NAAFI stores. Ours were all but exhausted, so I was given carte blanche and told not to return until I had acquired a sufficient supply. Bill Mabbott lent me a lorry and gave me an immense sum of money. By no means reluctantly I set out on a 'leg' of 200 miles for Tobruk.

The first evening I stopped near M'sus, unrecognisable in its new guise of advanced supply HQ, with the stilly peace of Fort Zinderneuf lost to the incessant roar of aeroplanes. The enterprise nearly ended in disaster that night when the quartermaster's henchmen managed to set fire to their lorry (which had a load of petrol), and we had a very tricky time until the RAF lent us some extra fire extinguishers. The lorry survived the incident and I prayed, unavailingly, that this might be the only blow of fate.

On the following morning everything went perfectly until midday, when I contrived to get both vehicles seemingly irrevocably bogged in a clay pan. We then spent three harrowing hours excavating a fair proportion of Libya before the impossible was somehow achieved and we could resume our journey – completely exhausted and covered from head to foot in revolting yellow mud.

I had resolved to try and reach a ruined fort called Charruba before dark. On the way we suddenly came onto the bank of a mysterious lake, unmarked on the map, a wonderful rose colour in the dying sun with the rare additional bonus of a sheltering acacia tree. The combination was not to be resisted and Smallridge cooked such a good supper that I sat up late to watch the moon rise, with a lot of incoherent philosophical thoughts about the East.

All next day we laboured along with my car boiling every five or ten miles, so that we had to turn round and drive rapidly into the following wind in an absurd, though effective, bid to cool it down. Tobruk, when we arrived, was shrouded in one of those stifling sandstorms to which it seemed especially prone. I slept, in comparative comfort, at the transit camp where my tentative and guarded questions about NAAFI elicited little useful information save that it was on the Bardia road and only open in the afternoons.

In the morning I paid a round of wearing and complicated visits to the post office and the field cashier and other strangleholds of bureaucracy. In the former I was lucky enough to meet Philip Flower of the Rifle Brigade. Philip was a sort of ADC, or 'bottle washer' as he called it, to Jock Campbell and I had seen him frequently during the past few weeks. We had many friends in common and laughed at the same things. He was now engaged in the same unofficial business as myself and we decided to join forces.

Before going to the NAAFI we took all our vehicles to have them filled with petrol. At the pump, to our surprise, the NCO refused to let us have any without a written order from someone or other. We then realised how far we had come back, as normally in the desert petrol was issued on demand. After much expostulation we were taken to see a Colonel Galley, who was comfortably established in a little white house. On his door was written 'Colonel Galley' – 'Knock twice and then enter'. 'I know', said Philip, 'what this man is going to be like.'

In appearance Galley resembled a crapulous fire-eater out of some inferior war cartoon. His mode of address was similar. He started off with a spate of abuse before we could even discover what it was all about. Gradually it transpired that we had infringed all his pettyfogging regulations in daring to demand petrol for what he called our 'nefarious journey'. We showed him our papers authorising our activities, we mentioned every general of whom we had ever heard. All in vain; Galley spluttered on. When it seemed that his powers were failing, the tale was taken up by an underling. We began to laugh. This clinched the matter and we were both dramatically put on open arrest and ordered to report to the area commander.

We overcame our irreverent mirth and reported to the officer concerned. He listened civilly to our account and then gave us a written order for our petrol requirements. He also asked us, with a smile, to apologise to Galley who was 'very particular in these matters'. We managed this disagreeable task without loss of dignity, though it was badly received. We subsequently discovered that Galley was a legend and every RASC officer that we met told us the most fantastic stories of his peculiar methods of administration.

Our luck was in at the NAAFI and we were able to buy large supplies of everything we needed. Rather than expose our cargo to the continued bumping of the desert route, we decided to use the coast road as far as south of Benghazi. It must also be admitted that we were both very anxious to see the settled part of Cyrenaica which was said to be very beautiful. Nor were we going to hurry.

As far as Derna the road ('Via Balbo') was as uninteresting as it had been between Alexandria and Tobruk. There was little to see except a few Italian police posts and the ugly remains of one or two battles, about which Philip, who was something of a desert veteran, was able to tell me; but it was pleasant to drive on a smooth surface again and the day passed swiftly. We approached Derna in the last hour of the sun. It was an enchanting surprise. The road, which for miles had run along the barren cliff tops, here very high, suddenly plunged down in a succession of corkscrew turns, and hundreds of feet below we saw the town lying on the edge of the Mediterranean, a startling vision of green and white – little boxlike houses and mosques, a mass of feathery palms and a Lilliputian harbour. One of the soldiers thought it looked as nice as Blackpool.

The serpentine descent was a marvel of road engineering, which we found everywhere, as we went on, to be of a very high order. The town itself, though scarred by bombing and raddled by the passage of armies, lost nothing on closer sight and I would have like to have idled for a week among its gardens, all ablaze with purple blossom. But we hastened to move on before nightfall, as we were told that it was bombed each night by German aeroplanes from Crete. We camped in a little cave, a few yards from the sea's edge, and slept to the sound of the lapping swell and distant anti-aircraft fire.

Our road the following day lay through a succession of deep rocky gorges, their precipitous sides dotted with cypress and maquis. Each little valley had a carpet of bright grass at the bottom with a stream of clear water running across it, and usually a biblical-looking Arab would be minding his flock of sheep and goats. But then the stony hills gradually died away and we emerged into the wide plain of Barce. This had been the biggest Italian settlement in Cyrenaica and had retained the fertility that in Roman times extended over the whole province, when it was called the 'granary of Rome'. It was organised on a communal basis, with each village surrounded by forty or fifty smallholdings of maybe four acres each. Every farmhouse was of a uniform pattern, painted white, and as the plain broadened out, one gained an overpowering impression of organised monotony at the sight of these regularly spaced pill boxes stretching into seeming infinity. All the villages, too, were of a pattern and contained little save a large church, an agricultural centre and innumerable placards of 'Viva il Duce!' They would be named after some Italian national hero such as d'Annunzio or Garibaldi, who deserved, and got, more ambitious commemoration elsewhere from their countrymen.

We missed seeing the amphitheatre at Apollonia as my car had broken a spring and we wanted to reach Barce that night. We found the town occupied by HQ of 4th Indian Division and I managed to get my car into one of their workshops. A new spring had to be made which would take a couple of days, so disdaining military hospitality we established ourselves in a little house outside the town, living in a hideous parlour and frowned upon by the portraits of the absent owner's forebears. We had collected a mass of assorted food, and some Chianti, and had some rare banquets – one roast kid would have done credit to Larue.

Barce, built under the Turkish regime, is quite large and contains a fort and a sizeable Arab population. We walked on the foothills behind the town and explored the deep caves that disappeared into their interior. The highest hill was crowned with a singular monument to the prowess of the Italian troops in the war of 1911 against Turkey. It consisted of a tall white tower with a form of lighthouse on the roof where, I imagine, a perpetual flame burned in peacetime. At the bottom of the tower was a chapel, in the best

Lourdes-sugar-icing-Carrara style, and below it a dismal crypt containing the bones and laudatory epitaphs of those who fell in the campaign. We also found a recent tablet which, according to our feeble translation, condemned the vandalism of the Australian troops who had barbarously defaced the vaults during the first advance to Benghazi. There was a wonderful view from the top and one could almost see the sea.

When my car was mended we started on the last part of our journey by road; south of Benghazi we would have to return to the desert. As we approached the sea again the country became drier and cultivation ceased except for a few fields round native villages. We passed two rather fine round walled towns, Tocra and Tolmetta, which command the Benghazi littoral, and reached the so-called capital city at noon.

Benghazi is surrounded by lagoons and spreading groves of palm trees and, although it lies very low, it has been magnificently planned in relation to land and water, and gives an impression of great light and space. At this time it had been fairly regularly bombed for over a year by both sides and was beginning to look rather shattered. I shudder to think of its appearance by the spring of 1943. Despite this it still had an air of grace and modernity. All the larger houses stood in gardens, and though of very plain architecture (well suited to the climate) looked very attractive with their dazzling white walls, green shutters and iron grilles and balconies.

We tried to enter the cathedral but it was reckoned unsafe and the doors were locked. Hardly any inhabitants were visible but the town major said there were twenty or thirty thousand Arabs still there, who had to be looked after. They formed a liability which both Axis and British forces were rather loath to accept with the other Dead Sea fruits of occupation. Marshal Graziani's lovely villa, which stood outside the town, we did not hear about until after we had left.

Leaving these shattered symbols of civilisation, we hurried on, by this time conscious of the fact that we had been away a long while. North of Agedabia we turned into the desert, rather sad that our holiday was over. I parted with Philip at divisional HQ and the following evening rejoined the regiment who were still on a patrol line – roughly where I had left them. The colonel told me that we would shortly be pulled out to refit as the cars had done over the statutory mileage and were due to be exchanged or overhauled. A week or so later we all moved back to the 'town' of M'sus, our task having been taken over by the 1st Support Group.

M'SUS AND A.M. BRITANNIQUES

13 Corps HQ was at M'sus and the colonel was told to prepare to take the entire regiment back to refit at Desert Railhead (about eighty miles south-east of Tobruk) but to leave behind a small composite squadron of the best-running cars as corps troops. To my pleasure, I was ordered to command this and I spent the morning of 25 January organising my little force.

About midday the electrifying news arrived that the Germans had broken through in strength in the south, had fought an action with 2nd Armoured Brigade at Saunnu (twenty to thirty miles away) and were now advancing on M'sus. The enemy had certainly timed their action very nicely, as new troops were everywhere taking over the front, and considerable chaos ensued. All the base installations at M'sus, aerodromes, hospitals, dumps and Corps HQ, began to pack and move off in frantic haste, and the air was thick with the dust of droves of lorries making their getaway.

The regiment managed to pack itself into its few remaining vehicles and I was left under the orders of Lieutenant-Colonel West who, with his battalion of Rajputana Rifles, was responsible for the evacuation of the place. He was a most urbane man, quite unmoved by the excitement, although he was in the unpleasant position of having insufficient transport in which to move his own troops. He greeted me with a wry reference to the 'captains and the kings'. I sent off my three troops to watch the threatened side, and they soon reported two large groups of tanks moving at speed towards the fort. Soon after this the first shells came over and this accelerated the departure northward of any few people remaining. Colonel West satisfied himself that the place was clear and loaded his battalion somehow onto a crazy circus of vehicles that he had impounded. I undertook to act as a rearguard and to keep an eye on the enemy.

They had halted and were indiscriminately shelling the fort and wadi. My three troops had gradually come in and Charles Gregson reported suddenly that a 'large body of black men' were wandering aimlessly about at the southern end of the wadi. I tore down there and found a hundred or so Indian Pioneers under the rather illogical command of a native doctor. They had been carelessly left behind by one of the 'captains and the kings', whom I cursed with every oath under the sun. Charles said the enemy tanks looked like moving again and, as the shelling had increased, I decided to move off as quickly as possible. I told him to remain where he was and called in the other two troops to my aid. By dint of many pantomime gestures and shouts of *'jildi'**, we loaded the Indians into our cars and my two lorries and made off rapidly to the north, looking like *'tableaux vivants* of Empire' at the Lord Mayor's Show.

Charles coordinated his movements to ours and told me, on the air, that we had moved only just in time as the Germans had nearly encircled the place and we were escaping

* An invaluable word: strictly speaking the Hindu word is *'jaldi'* meaning to hurry. The 12th Lancers had not served in India since early in the century but it was firmly in the regimental vocabulary, by this time corrupted to *'jillo'*. Soldiers were often asked to get a 'jillo on', meaning to move rapidly in whatever they were doing.

through the only gap. On reaching an area of comparative safety I endeavoured to regain my breath and balance. The worst was now over and I shortly received orders to move right back to Charruba, where it seemed I would find most of the British Army. On the way we commandeered two 'swanning' lorries and packed the Indians into them; we also gave tow to an ambulance which had broken down. In it was the gallant Doctor 'Stinker' Dowell, who was now serving with divisional headquarters, preparing for capture with his cargo of wounded men. He was more than relieved to discover our identity.

At Charruba I managed to pass the Indian Pioneers on to someone else and then looked around for a source of orders. The 2nd Armoured Brigade were about to take me under command when I received a message from the colonel that I was on no account to get embroiled there but was to come back to Mechili and rejoin him at 13 Corps HQ. When I arrived there the following afternoon, I found that I was again to stay with that formation, but only as long as was tactically necessary in view of the poor condition of our vehicles. That evening we said goodbye to the regiment (bound for Railhead), though not before I had been able to obtain Neil as my second in command. He had just come up from Cairo and I was unfeignedly glad to have him with me. It was rather exciting to have an independent command and I felt very exhilarated.

John Harding was BGS of 13 Corps and I received my orders from him. He was a cool and able person with a charm and good humour which he extended to everyone under all conditions, and with none of that gradation of manners, according to rank, so common to the higher staff officer. In all conscience things were in rather a desperate plight at this time and I fancy he was getting little or no sleep, but he managed to achieve all that was required with a courteous efficiency which was very striking. He kept me busy, as my troops had to do long trips to link up with outlying brigades, but after a few days the situation stabilised and it became a little easier – to my considerable relief as I was rather worried about the cars.

We bivouacked alongside Corps HQ and I was connected to G. Ops by telephone. On our fourth or fifth night there, I was rung up in the small hours by the BGS who told me that HQ were moving back, within a few minutes, to Tmimi, but that I was to stay and come under the command of the Polish Brigade, who would have arrived by dawn, and subsequently under that of the Free French who would succeed them. As far as I could gather, Mechili (which consisted of a ruined fort, some minefields, a well and some high ground) was to become a bastion in the new line and was to be strongly held. I told Neil that I had a feeling that we were about to be involved in something that was not quite our kind of warfare – and I remembered Mick Lindsay's squadron of KDGs who were caught in the siege of Tobruk and remained there for some months. The subalterns all thought it was very funny and wondered whether they would have to live on their shoe leather and desert rats, but I was not so happy about it.

Dawn broke to find us surrounded by Poles, all talking with immense volubility. I went off to find their brigadier, hoping that he would have an interpreter or could at least talk a little French. General Kopanski, when I discovered him, addressed me in such beautiful, almost Shakespearean, English that I felt ashamed of my shallow colloquialisms. Later I learnt that he was a man of considerable intellectual eminence.

Beyond our exchange of courtesies I had little further to do with the Polish Brigade; the Free French soon arrived and their commander assumed control of both forces. It was fortunate that the Luftwaffe was temporarily inactive, as Mechili was packed with men and vehicles and presented a perfect bombing target. Members of the Spears Mission were attached to the French and this was supposed to facilitate our relations with them. In fact we found the Mission members an uncooperative clique, disliked by both sides and, we decided, interested only in their own comfort. Accordingly I made contact with the 3ème Bureau (Operations), with one of whose officers, Capitaine Marti, I dealt directly and received the greatest kindness and attention. We also acquired the services of a delightful English intelligence officer, Fitzgerald, who was rather at a loose end and anxious not to be associated with the Spears Mission.

Later that afternoon I was introduced to the French general, de Larminat. He was very pleasant to me, complimented me on my indifferent French and asked me to a conference that evening, in the meantime requiring me to look after *'la surêté eloignée'*. This gave me a free hand and I sent out patrols ten or twenty miles, to give good warning of any enemy approach. The general's ADC, a bumptious New York corset-maker called Laurelle, insisted on accompanying one of these, but the troop leader, John Henderson, managed to frighten him during the journey to such an extent that thereafter his duties kept him permanently at HQ. Meanwhile I established the squadron outside the perimeter, which was being fortified, and throughout our attachment managed to remain there despite blandishments to draw us within.

At the conference, in his luxurious caravan, the pontifical General de Larminat treated us to a tactical exposition that would have done credit to Jomini, and which was far above the heads of most of his audience, especially myself. He was one of those fiercely intellectual, almost mystical, French officers whose minds soar through clouds of the abstract with only rare descents to earth, a type of soldier whom one encounters seldom in the British Army. I hoped fervently that there would be some interpretation of the words of the Master, some lifting aside of the veil that hid his meaning and I was heartily thankful when General Koenig, his second in command, gave a clear summary in a few laconic phrases. Koenig, the practical antithesis of his academic superior, had a fine record of twenty years or more in the French Legion and was to win glory six months later at Bir Hacheim.

He confirmed what I knew, namely that 'Force F' (Free French and Polish Brigades) was to hold Mechili in the event of a German attack until such time as the British line further eastwards had stabilised. General Koenig emphasised that this might have to be to the last round, in which case he did not doubt that they would die like Frenchmen, but in the meantime they were to concentrate on perfecting the defences of Mechili. 'Notre collègue, M. le chef d'escadron des auto-mitrailleuses britanniques' – I was so overcome by this magnificent title that I nearly missed returning the courteous bow that the general directed towards me – would keep them appraised of the future moves of the enemy and, knowing the distinguished arm of the service to which I belonged, the general did not doubt that this vital task would be acquitted with no little ability and gallantry. The conference dissolved in great amity and I hurried away before it was dark.

The French part of Force F contained some exceedingly diverse elements and we had much interest and entertainment in studying them during the next few weeks – they were fully representative of the many races of the French Colonial Empire. The staff were very hard-working and efficient, most of them Frenchmen who had been in business in the Mediterranean or the Levant. The *chef de l'état-major,* a Jew from Lille, was the only regular officer. The HQ personnel included two English girls, drivers of the general's cars, a few sailors and a horde of Cochin Chinese, who did all the dirty work.

Three battalions of the Foreign Legion formed the backbone of the brigade. They were very fine troops of whom about half were French. The remainder were of all nationalities under the sun, even to a few renegade Englishmen, whom we could never persuade to speak of their past. The commander of these battalions was a Georgian prince named Amaklavari, a remarkable swashbuckling figure and, I think, a genuine fire-eater. He was a wonderful shot and was said to be able to bring down snipe and quail with a rifle, though we were never privileged to see his prowess in this particular field. He had very few officers but I remember very distinctly his signals officer, a German of about fifty who had been at a cadet school with Rommel. I have never seen men dig like the Legion. In the course of a few hours they disappeared completely beneath the desert.

There were three or four batteries of gunners, with very assorted weapons manned by Bretons and Senegalese, both of whom were quite unintelligible, and a dashing naval anti-aircraft outfit whose caps, with their red bobbles, added a touch of musical-comedy colour to the scene. Any aeroplane was fair game to them and after a few days all our own aircraft gave Mechili a wide berth.

Then there was the Bataillon Pacifique. This rather unfortunately named organisation puzzled us for a long time and we vaguely imagined it to be some kind of non-combatant labour corps. We did not actually see it for a week and did not like to ask questions about it, fearing to commit some solecism of military manners. It turned out to be a band of luckless Polynesians who had been wrenched away from their languorous Tahiti to fight for a cause of which they can have understood little. Their officers were also locally raised and were a singular collection of Gauguinesque beachcombers, all desperately shy. They had not yet been tried under fire and were very anxious not to smirch the traditions of their island.

And finally there was Bob, one of the more colourful figures that I met during the war. He attached himself particularly to us and his capacity for gin was such that Neil had to go off to Tobruk within a few days for fresh supplies. He prided himself on his English, which was that of an inferior Marseilles pimp, and on his love of England which seemed very genuine, as he had frequently crossed the Channel to ride at Olympia and had been very hospitably entertained.

His English friends had called him Bob and by this name he liked to be called, though his full title was Chef d'escadron Robert de Kerzauzon de Penandef. He was a Breton, a beautifully built man with an insolent brown face crowned by a flamboyant red kepi heavily laced with gold (a relic of his Spahi days). In age about forty-five, he had been, between the two wars, a very social soldier, usually stationed at Senlis or somewhere equally convenient for Paris and for polo at Bagatelle. Occasionally he had ventured abroad in search of glory and financial recuperation and, by his blaze of medal ribbons, appeared to have been successful in the former. He was in the habit of spending most of the day sitting in my car and recounting his many adventures, amorous and otherwise, and making us laugh. Stimulating as his company was, I sometimes wondered if he had any work to do and what his exact position was in Force F. To my rather tentative inquiries he would reply with a wealth of evasive rhodomontade, suggesting that he preferred not to speak on this subject.

Fitzgerald finally enlightened me with a few facts that he had collected from some of the staff. Bob had started the war in Syria as pro-Vichy, like virtually all his friends. At the end of that campaign he had missed the boat or aeroplane which was to take him back to France through some mysterious *malheur* (variously believed to be a prolonged celebration, a naval officer's wife or a sudden illness) and Bob, to use his own expression, was 'beetched'. However, after a few hours' thought he took the logical course and offered his services to the Free French, who accepted them with a somewhat bad grace. Since then he had been doing odd jobs and had lately been sent to de Larminat who would not, or could not, give him a post and he was therefore at present a passenger. Poor Bob used to become rather maudlin after half a bottle of gin, declaring that he was the plaything of fate and that never again would come a chance for glory. We would make sympathetic noises and fill his glass, and soon he would recapture one of his high moods of storytelling and say 'Did evaire I tell you about the sister of the Spanish chargé d'affaires? Migod [all one word] how she love me' – and so on.

We stayed at Mechili three weeks without any excitements. I furnished my usual patrols but there was no enemy within thirty miles, though we heard that they were filtering through the hills east of Derna. The French were wildly enthusiastic over the use of minefields and laid them down indiscriminately, usually without markings, so that going through the perimeter became a tortuous and perilous business. We lived well, as they had excellent rations, which included rum and wine; Sergeant Darraugh, who was my SQMS, used to bring back large quantities of these stimulants which were very welcome in the cold weather.

At the end of this period we heard that a defended line had been established at Gazala and that the Mechili position was to be abandoned. The prospect of a withdrawal gave a rare opportunity for some highly complex planning on the part of de Larminat and we were inundated with orders and diagrams. It was finally arranged that the force should be split into five columns which would leave the position at timed intervals. This scheme, despite some uncalled-for criticism on my part, was a very neat piece of work.

Bob, to his delight, was given a post of honour, the command of the last column. This was called, in the orders, 'la cinquième colonne' but it was regarded as a joke in bad taste at Bob's expense (he suspected the Jewish *chef de l'état-major*) and its name was changed to 'la colonne mobile'. It contained some cadet anti-tank gunners, a battery of Breton artillery, a company of assorted infantry, some of the naval ack-ack guns and my own squadron. Bob was as happy as a child and spent his time in giving tactical lectures and drawing diagrams in the sand.

We left Mechili in style, with the column commander standing on the outside of my armoured car so that he could survey his force. Spread out over two or three miles, it looked very imposing. I had two troops a long way behind, guarding our rear. That evening Geoffrey Nares, who commanded one of them, had an exciting skirmish with four German armoured cars. He saw them off and rescued an officer and some men of the KDGs* who had been captured. Fitzgerald had been on this trip and returned with a glowing account of Geoffrey's gallantry. I subsequently tried to obtain Geoffrey a decoration for this and Fitzgerald made the French send in a citation as well. Geoffrey was very amused when he heard that this started with the words 'Cet officier, calme et digne en face d'un feu meurtrier . . .'

We stopped that night under a prominent hill called Ezeizat, and on the morning rejoined the rest of the force on the Gazala line. Here I received a signal to return to the regiment at Railhead and we started as soon as possible, after a polite round of valedictions and a rather emotional stirrup cup with Bob.

INTERLUDE

At Talatta, a stretch of the desert encumbered with railway lines and rolling stock, I found the regiment refitting. It appeared that I was odd man out as the colonel wanted to keep Neil in the desert now that he had arrived, and he thought I had better go back to Cairo and command the Details until a squadron was vacant. I was quite ready to return for a short period but I did not wish to stay there for long, although I had no wish to displace anyone from his present position. There was a party going off to draw new cars and I travelled back with them.

The road approaching Cairo is very dull until one suddenly sees the Pyramids appearing over the sand dunes. A little further on a vision of the delta suddenly springs on one, a

*The King's Dragoon Guards were also equipped with armoured cars.

seeming paradise of trees and greenery with no sign of Cairo save the fairy dome and minarets of the Citadel, backed by the dull brown Mokattam Hills. This view never failed to thrill me when returning after months of nothing save monochrome gravel.

It was pleasant to be back in civilisation and I was very comfortable at the armoured car mess at Abbassia and enjoyed myself a lot until I had to retire to bed with 'flu and very malignant 'gyppy tummy'. When I recovered I discovered that I had extraordinarily little work to do, beyond attending to correspondence, visiting the wounded and keeping an eye on the training of newly arrived drafts; all of which never took more than three hours a day. Alan Carson, who was recovering from bad bomb shock, was meant to help me but in view of the scarcity of work I sent him off on leave to the better air of Palestine.

A friend kindly lent me the use of his ponies and I was able to ride out into the desert in the early morning when it was still fairly fresh. Cairo was very entertaining to visit for a few days when on leave, as one always saw a lot of friends and the shortness of the stay enabled one to spend money rather lavishly without too much harm to the bank account. But for any length of time it was seriously expensive and one became very bored with the permanent garrison of staff officers who held the fortress of Middle East HQ. I soon began to bombard Peter Burne with letters demanding a recall to the desert – very unreasonably, as I knew he had no place to give me.

In the meantime I looked around for alternative employment. Bill Carr, who had been my squadron leader before the war, and who was always a good friend to me, was now commanding 22nd Armoured Brigade and to him I poured out my woes one night at dinner. He promised to find some kind of job for me as liaison officer on his staff, but a few days later said that Willoughby Norrie (30 Corps) had heard that I was 'on the market' and had applied for me. Bill thought I would go there as he, a mere brigadier, had little say where a corps commander was concerned. While I was digesting this news I was suddenly despatched on a three-week tactical course in Palestine, but managed to extract a promise from Middle East HQ that I would be sent somewhere on my return.

The small tactical school lay among orange groves at Karkur, about twenty miles inland from Haifa. It was excellently conducted and catered for the needs of prospective squadron, company and battery commanders, teaching something of the latest use of all arms. It was completely up to date and au fait with the newest developments from the desert. We toured the country extensively on TEWTs and saw something of Allenby's battlefields. It was delightful to be in good air and green surroundings again and I walked a lot on the hills with Tony Johnson of the 4th Hussars. At the weekends we went into Haifa to dine at one of the very good restaurants run by German and Hungarian émigrés.

Back in Cairo I found that all my difficulties were over as Arthur Gemmell had received a staff appointment and I was to return to the desert immediately to command 'C' Squadron. So within a day or two Smallridge and I and my multifarious belongings were packed into the desert train and were clanking towards Fort Capuzzo, to where Railhead had now advanced. It was an appalling journey, with sand swirling into the cattle trucks, and I was enduring perpetual thirst, the aftermath of the 11th Hussars' farewell to Cairo on leaving for Mosul. It had been a very 'old-fashioned' evening and Shepheard's Hotel was a shambles at the close of the festivities. An ugly incident had nearly occurred when a box containing the uniform of a Turkish plenipotentiary had come into acute danger during Bill Wainman's practical demonstration of fire-fighting in the entrance hall. I recall large jets of water shooting all over the building to the vociferous despair of the Berberene servants. The despair of the assistant manager was inaudible as he was rolled up, out of danger, in a carpet.

From Capuzzo we travelled through days of lorry-hopping to HQ 1st Armoured Division. Here I was greeted in a most congratulatory manner and discovered, to my great surprise, that I had received a bar to the MC for the M'sus incident, largely thanks to a eulogistic report from Colonel West.

The regiment I found due for a further mechanical refit, as in my absence they had been very busy on the Gazala line. This time they were returning to the Delta to re-equip thoroughly and to get some leave – most of them had had five consecutive months in the desert. 'C' Squadron, however, with the best cars, was to remain behind under command of 22nd Armoured Brigade until it could be relieved by one of the others. I found Edward Mann and all the rest of them in admirable spirits and quite unperturbed at the thought of another month or so in the desert. Once again I was a fairly independent agent, answerable only to a brigadier who knew all about armoured cars. The regiment gave us the best of everything they had left and we moved off to join 22nd Armoured Brigade near Bir Harmat.

KNIGHTSBRIDGE AND BACK

The 22nd Armoured Brigade had preceded the rest of the 1st Armoured Division to Egypt and had fought with some distinction at the Battle of Sidi Rezegh in November 1941, under Brigadier Scott-Cockburn. Bill Carr was then commanding the Sharpshooters (the other two regiments in the brigade were 2nd Royal Gloucester Hussars and 3rd County of London Yeomanry) but had been quite severely wounded. He received a well-earned DSO and in the early part of 1942 was given command of the brigade. The latter, with 2nd Armoured Brigade and 22nd Guards Brigade, formed the 1st Armoured Division under Herbert Lumsden.

It was obvious that Rommel, having built up his reserves in front of the Gazala-Bir Hacheim line, would shortly attack, and this was accurately forecast by the Intelligence branch for the end of May. Along this line lay a long series of British minefields. Between Gazala and Knightsbridge 13 Corps (Lieutenant-General Gott) were well dug in, while at Hacheim the Free French (now under Koenig) were equally well entrenched. If the Germans broke through the minefields in the lower part of the northern half (the geography of the upper part precluded this), it was hoped to lure them into fighting an armoured battle at Knightsbridge, where the ground was advantageous to us. To make it more so, the Guards Brigade dug a defended position, or 'box', there and this was to form the pivot of manoeuvre of Herbert Lumsden's armoured brigades. If the Germans broke through the southern half, or by-passed Hacheim, the 7th Armoured Division was in a good position to meet them, and in any of these contingencies each armoured division was admirably placed for aiding the other. It seemed certain that in any attempt on Tobruk the Germans would have to fight at Knightsbridge and GHQ prophesied that the breakthrough would be to the west of this point.

By this time the armoured brigades had one squadron of American General Grant tanks per regiment, armed with a 75 mm gun, and they were also in progress of being equipped with 6-pounder anti-tank guns. It was reckoned that we had tank parity with the Germans and everyone was very confident over the coming issue.

For the two or three weeks preceding the battle we were kept very busy reconnoitring the ground and, on Bill Carr's particular insistence, getting to know the different formations and commanders. During the operation I had constantly to relay wireless messages and send troops to find different units, and without this knowledge it would have been impossible. We were all tremendously impressed with the brigade, which was a masterpiece of smooth running in all its complex component parts, and anything we required was provided with commendable swiftness. In accordance with the expected breakthrough west of Knightsbridge I had emergency stations for my troops in this area, to which they were to go on the alarm. We were visited once or twice by Herbert Lumsden, very imperturbable and very active, and frequently saw him quartering the desert in a low open car.

We were in the habit of standing to for an hour before dawn. On 27 May we had finished this and were having breakfast when the alarm signal came over the air. I immediately despatched three of my troops to their positions and awaited events. I remember sitting on top of my car with Edward watching the brigade form up, ready to move to Knightsbridge. Suddenly, to our astonishment, we heard firing to the south and a minute or two later a cloud of vehicles appeared over that horizon five or six miles away, and coming on at a great pace. Immediately the whole brigade changed front, to meet them, a fine piece of manoeuvring involving 150 tanks, two battalions of motorised infantry and about a dozen different batteries of guns. Edward's rear link wireless (to brigade HQ) was a babel of conversation and we could gather little from it, but it was apparent that the enemy had not taken the presaged course, but had skirted Hacheim. What we could not fathom was what had happened to the 7th Armoured Division, and why we had had practically no notice of the enemy's advance.

By this time battle was nearly joined between the two forces and shells were falling everywhere. We were now frantically busy on the wireless as I had to send my troops round onto the enemy flanks as well as attempt to gain contact with the 7th Armoured Division. All this, and the thickening dust, prevented us from seeing all the battle but what little we did see was very thrilling.

Our General Grant tanks had been provided with canvas

frames so that from a distance they looked like lorries. They were fitted with a quick-release mechanism, and at a given moment they dramatically shed their disguises and opened fire, to the vast surprise of the Germans. The dust and confusion now became intense. Sometimes we were able to catch a glimpse of a tank blowing up and once we had an excellent view of the enemy anti-tank gunners coming into action with lightning rapidity. All the time our bombers were going over under a heavy fighter screen.

About midday there was a lull in the fighting and as my own situation had clarified itself, I went off in search of Bill Carr's HQ and to discover what had happened to 7th Armoured Division. The troops that I had sent to find it had only encountered scattered units and its fate was still unknown.

Brigade HQ consisted of a couple of armoured cars and a tank, and a throng of officers bent over maps and the wireless. The brigadier was very busy but his intelligence officer, Esmond Baring, gave me all the news.

That morning, before dawn, the Germans had come around Hacheim in a very strong force and had overrun the greater part of 7th Armoured Division, including its HQ. The 4th Armoured Brigade had been caught in close leaguer, with the rising sun behind them, and had been badly knocked about, the 8th Hussars being practically annihilated. The divisional commander, General Messervy, had been captured but had since made his escape, and the whole force was now re-forming further back, where new tanks and crews had been assembled. The latter operation had been rather complicated by a further German column making for Sidi Rezegh, but this had now been dealt with, and it was hoped that the division would be up that night or the following morning. No one quite knew how it was that it had been surprised, as it had adequate outposts and reconnaissance screens in front, and it was generally thought to have been due to a break in wireless communications.

Esmond said that the enemy were now trying to break through the Knightsbridge minefields, from the west, but had suffered very heavy casualties at the hands of the Guards Brigade whose troglodyte existence was completely unexpected. Our brigade was shortly to move back into that area to join up with 2nd Armoured Brigade, the recent action having been successful, although we had had some casualties. Meanwhile the Free French were staving off a tremendous onslaught at Hacheim.

That night a very heavy battle developed but by the following evening Herbert Lumsden had three armoured brigades under command (2nd, 4th and 22nd – in all probably about 400 tanks) and had enticed the enemy into the desired position. Everyone was very excited.

We had a singularly trying time. Bill Carr had told me always to remain near his HQ, which meant that we never stopped moving. He was a very dashing leader and, during the big battle, liked to be up near the front of his troops. It made both Edward and me very conscious of the thin armour on our machines as compared with that of the tanks.

My outlying troops were still very busy linking up with other formations and watching the enemy flanks and the air was never quiet for a moment. John Richardson had the misfortune to run into some anti-tank guns in a sandstorm and lost a car and a man, but otherwise we were unscathed, though rather tired. The Germans put in constant Stuka attacks but our anti-aircraft barrage was very strong and, anyway, they no longer came very low nor bombed with any great precision.

The next three days or so were very strenuous and critical, with fierce fighting day and night. An incredibly thick dust storm delayed the issue for some hours, during which trying to find the enemy was made extremely unpleasant. Luckily for us he had not moved and shortly after we located him the storm lifted and our tanks could again attack.

Refuelling was a nightmare as it was impossible to relieve

my troops until after dark and they then had to come five or ten miles in to me, through minefields, taking their bearings on Very lights which everyone else was sending up. Alan Carson was now my transport officer and somehow always reached me with the replacement lorry, though I was frequently only able to give him the scantiest indication of my whereabouts.

One very jumpy night we were in leaguer with brigade HQ and hoping for an hour or two of sleep. It soon became obvious, however, that a large portion of the Wehrmacht were occupying adjacent ground and we had to make a rather undignified escape, which ended in all our own people opening an intensive fire on us.

One's life was divided between a map and a wireless, in the midst of a sandy shell-laden confusion, with jangled nerves, hardly any sleep and a monumental thirst. Our principal items of diet seemed to be tinned fruit and black coffee but I suppose we must have eaten something more solid. At least we could claim that this particular action had been outstandingly successful for us. A great number of enemy tanks were destroyed and intercepted enemy wireless messages showed that their supply echelons had been badly dislocated by bombing and that many units were almost out of petrol. Everything was prepared to exploit this situation.

Our plan, in brief, was to drive through the minefields and then turn up towards the coast and cut the Germans off. I had seen Herbert Lumsden quite a lot in the last few days, a striking example of what a general should be, very cool and certain, and civil to everyone. He now told me to get extra loads of petrol, as he wished to send all the armoured cars he had miles behind the enemy and let them run amok among his lines of communication.

The new plan found little favour at GHQ who were determined on stabilising for a week before thinking of advancing. It also appeared that Herbert Lumsden was temporarily in disgrace (from excessive use, one gathered, of the Nelson touch) and General Messervy, recovered from his adventures, took control of the armoured forces. This rather depressed us all and even more so when during the following days our armour was gradually worn away, in driblets, instead of being retained for a massed onslaught. In this period we lost our golden opportunity of taking the initiative, while allowing Rommel time to recoup for his successful thrust to Tobruk, by which time we had few armoured troops to resist him.

My squadron's activity now increased, as the amount of small actions gave us an increasing number of situations with which to maintain touch. Sergeant Robinson, one of the troop leaders, did some magnificent work recovering nearly 200 wounded prisoners of war who had been abandoned by the Italians. He made journey after journey to bring them in, always under heavy shell and anti-tank fire. Most of the prisoners were in a very bad way, and almost dead of thirst and shock, and they most certainly owed their lives to his action – for which he was awarded the DCM. He was a first-rate, highly intelligent NCO, who later on became my squadron sergeant-major and finished up as regimental sergeant-major.

The 22nd Armoured Brigade were being given a few days' rest, so we were handed over to the GSO1 of 7th Armoured Division, not a very sympathetic character. He had become a little shaken by the turn of events and on the slightest provocation would move Divisional HQ miles to the rear, so that it became completely inaccessible. On one occasion he went so far as to fall back to Corps HQ, from which he was summarily propelled towards the battle again by Willoughby Norrie. In the course of these counter marchings I had had a difference of opinion with him and had been placed under arrest, which confirmed the resemblance I saw between him and Colonel Galley. Presumably I am still under arrest as the order was never rescinded. However, soon afterwards 'A' Squadron arrived from Cairo to relieve us.

We now started moving as rapidly eastwards down the coast road as our rather unsound cars permitted. At Army HQ I had to stop for the necessary movement orders and, I fear, had rather high words with a South African staff officer who wanted to divert us across the desert because the road was urgently required for westbound traffic. In view of our shaky condition I knew this would be risky, but I compromised by travelling initially at the side of the road. After ten or fifteen miles I reverted to it as traffic of any kind was almost non-existent.

At Sollum we halted for a while and we all plunged into a clean and clear Mediterranean. Edward then went on ahead, at a rapid pace, to prepare our arrival in Cairo. Between Amrya and Cairo we met the remainder of the regiment moving up and I stopped to see the colonel. Everyone thought we had had a hard gruelling – which was gratifying – and Peter Burne told me to stay long enough to give everyone adequate leave and to re-equip the squadron completely.

We had a further problem on the journey back. Petrol in the Middle East was supplied in fragile four-gallon tins, two of them being encased in a flimsy wooden frame. The wastage was quite appalling and we all tried to equip ourselves with captured enemy jerrycans which were strong and did not leak. Armoured car regiments, of necessity, always carried with each squadron headquarters a reserve of petrol in what were called, with justification, the 'fighting lorries'. In 'C' squadron we had managed to equip the latter almost entirely with jerrycans and I was horrified when stopped on this journey by the Military Police who had orders to remove them all. I had no intention of relinquishing them, especially as within a short time we were to return to the desert. I managed to bluff through a series of obstructions, all the way to Cairo, and was finally able to retain them, thanks largely to a friend in GHQ who had destroyed the signals complaining of my illicit activities.

At Abbassia Edward had arranged such a perfect reception

that we might have been a foreign embassy instead of a dirty collection of soldiers. That night, fresh from the Turkish bath and the barber, the officers of 'C' squadron sat very complacently under General Kleber's tree in the garden of Shepheard's drinking, with gusto, indifferent champagne.

The next day I sent most of the officers and men away on leave and went to Middle East HQ, where the AFV branch was now under Dick McCreery, my first commanding officer. Despite my shortcomings as a young officer, he took a continuing kindly interest in me and was not only more than helpful on this occasion, including inviting me to dinner with a mass of general officers, but after the war asked me to come to Vienna, where he was commander-in-chief, as his personal assistant. In some ways I wish I had accepted, but I was going to be married and I also thought I was far too much out of touch with military matters.

Under his direction the department was functioning most efficiently, and I was told to 'draw' a complete new squadron – the latest pattern of armoured cars, good lorries, three Jeeps (these were then something quite new) and an excellent Ford utility car. The week went all too quickly and before the joys of civilisation were fully realised we were once more on the desert road, but equipped *en prince* for a long spell. We were sufficiently veteran to know what was required and the subsequent months, though arduous, were made easier by the comforts with which we had provided ourselves. Herbert Lumsden had always rightly said that it took a fool to be uncomfortable. We had adequate supplies of whisky, a fair amount of tinned food over and above the rations and Edward Mann had discovered that eggs would keep quite a long time if packed in sand. In addition we also acquired some hens who did not lay too badly despite a life of constant movement and a diet of army biscuits. Also a rather nice mongrel dog joined us at that time and certainly travelled on as far as Algeria with the squadron.

While we were in Cairo the news of the fighting had

become very alarming, culminating in the fall of Tobruk. It appeared that our troops were now falling back towards Mersa Matruh. On the way up we passed an endless stream of vehicles (mostly RAF) moving towards Alexandria, which told its own tale.

I finally located HQ 1st Armoured Division somewhere south-west of Matruh. Here I talked to Christopher Sinclair, the GSO2, who told me that Peter Burne and Gerald Churchill had been captured, having been sent to an incorrect rendezvous while serving with 10th Indian Division. While I was digesting this startling and gloomy information, the general arrived, thin and tired, but as serene as ever. He said he would keep me under his own hand for the moment until the situation cleared, rather than send me to 10th Indian Division to join the rest of the regiment. I was very thankful for this and was even more so when I subsequently heard the adventures of the other squadrons who were serving with that formation.

Two days and nights passed, occupied in rather difficult reconnaissance, as we were now in an area which was so far back that no adequate maps of it existed. There was also the added danger of our forgotten minefields which were here strewn about in some profusion. There appeared to be little armour left, save a very depleted 22nd Armoured Brigade, and the division mostly consisted of armoured cars and the remains of 7th Motor Brigade. The latter had recently distinguished itself though its young commander, Hugo Garmoyle, had been tragically killed.

Bill Carr asked to have us back and we rejoined his headquarters one morning while it was still dark. He, too, was very tired and it was obvious that the unexploited victory at Knightsbridge still lay heavily on his mind. That evening brought the prospect of an imminent withdrawal of eighty to a hundred miles. John Richardson, burnt so black by the sun that we called him the 'wallah', again had the misfortune to run into the enemy in the quickening dark and had two men wounded. It was a very inopportune moment – like most moments at this period – as there were no ambulances near and the brigade was already forming up in close order for the night march. Luckily we managed to put both casualties onto the back of a Cruiser tank, a vehicle that travelled very evenly over hard going, and they were finally evacuated to the rear without too much discomfort.

That night will always live in my memory. We were at the rear of the brigade, which was moving in five parallel columns, and although there was a bright moon we could see little owing to the immense clouds of sand raised by the tanks. Consequently we sometimes approached sudden dips and declivities in the ground at too fast a pace and the cars got an appalling shaking and nearly overturned. I began to wonder how many would be running in the morning but miraculously they all survived. The rear troops were certain that we were being dogged by enemy reconnaissance elements but we must have shaken them off by the morning.

The dawn found us still pounding along, bruised and bleary-eyed, but having covered a big mileage. With the coming of the light I spread my troops out over five to ten miles to cover our rear and a little later we halted to cook a much-needed breakfast. Brigade HQ looked very woebegone, as well they might. We were feeling indifferent enough after three sleepless nights and this had been their seventh.

While I was there a message came from division putting me under command of the Royals, and I switched my rear link wireless over to their frequency. They gave me a patrol line to watch and we had a comparatively easy day, helped by the arrival of the faithful Alan with a bag of mail. That evening orders arrived to move back a certain distance and to take up fresh positions at dawn. We were now in the narrowing bottleneck between the sea and the Qattara depression, and I realised that there was no great liberty of manoeuvre if we were cut off. Although I did not know it the enemy was already east of us in other areas.

At midnight we stopped and leaguered in a shallow saucer to get a little sleep. I was soon aroused by the sentry and at once heard an ominous noise of moving vehicles. Peering over the slight ridge we could see, in the light of the moon, a mass of tanks and lorries travelling east at about 800 yards' distance – a very eerie sight. It took no expert in identification to perceive that they were German. I resolved to remain quiet in our protecting saucer and to move on when the way was clear.

Shortly before dawn seemed propitious and I shaped a course to avoid following their tracks too closely. Owing to the great pace at which they were moving some of their lorries had dropped out of the column and had stopped, either from engine trouble or from the driver's fatigue. We managed to collect a nice little bag of very surprised Germans (most of whom were indulging in a short 'kip') and set all the lorries on fire. As they all contained either water or petrol, I hoped their destruction would cause acute embarrassment to certain sections of the Deutsches Afrika Korps.

Geoffrey Nares was navigating for me and had to compete with a very complex course. We had to keep changing direction to avoid not only the enemy, but also a series of deep, inaccessible wadis of which there were no traces on our indifferent maps. About midday the Royals, who were making an equally difficult withdrawal, gave me information on the air of a 'zone of safety' or defended line for which we should now steer. This was what afterwards became the Alamein line.

Throughout that afternoon, although we covered a considerable distance tacking we made very little easting and I became more and more worried over our chances of reaching the zone of safety. We ran into Toby Wetherly's squadron of KDGs, undergoing the same difficulties, and joined forces with it. By 5 p.m. our position had greatly improved when we were suddenly subjected to an intense bombardment from all sides. From what little I knew of bursting shells I surmised that these came from British and German guns and that we were in a sort of no man's land. Toby and I had a frenzied consultation and resolved to dash for our own side, risking mines and anti-tank guns. Providence obligingly took a hand with a protecting sandstorm, under cover of which we travelled to safety and emerged behind our own guns and infantry. I never felt so exhausted in my life.

We stayed with the Royals a few days, comparing our recent adventures and doing some light patrol work. One evening Mark Wyndham's troop was with the 22nd Armoured Brigade again and through him I received the melancholy news of the death of Frank Arkwright, while commanding the Sharpshooters. Frank had been adjutant when I joined in 1937 and I had much admired him as a soldier and a man. He and his wife had always been very kind to me; both had a keenly developed sense of the ridiculous and I always associated their house with gaiety and laughter. Frank would have gone a long way in the service – he had previously been GSO1 to Herbert Lumsden – and he was a born soldier with a very quick brain and the gift of being completely unruffled by any persons or circumstances. It was rather a depressing finale to our withdrawal.

Within a few days we rejoined the regiment (I had by now not served with it for nearly five months) which had had a very hard three weeks during the delaying action along the coast road. Owing to the splitting up of the squadrons at different intervals the personnel was rather mixed up, but we now found time to reorganise ourselves. I at last received all my own people back with my original officers, Edward Mann, Mark Wyndham, Robin Brockbank, John Stimpson, Geoffrey Nares and Alan Carson (who incidentally was the head of the school during the latter part of my rather inglorious stay at Rugby). Two first-class sergeants acted as troop leaders, Maguire* and Robinson, and the latter became

*Bob Maguire was later to be commissioned in the field and decorated with both the MM and MC.

squadron sergeant-major when the invaluable SSM Ellen, to whom I can never pay sufficient tribute, was promoted RQMS. I could not have had a better squadron or more delightful companions and I was happy with them all. They were all in their early twenties except for Geoffrey and Alan who were my own age. SSM Ellen was a greybeard of thirty-five and Maguire about thirty.

We were now a very young regiment as George Kidston, our new colonel, was only thirty-five or six. George, with whom I had served in my early days, had been away from us for some time having been adjutant and, on the outbreak of war, second-in-command of the Sharpshooters. He had recently been commanding the KDGs and we were relieved when we learnt that he was not to stay there but to return to us. He was a particularly charming person and an efficient soldier, a combination not all that common. Although by now he knew very few of us he quickly made himself respected and liked and proved a most successful CO. To me he was always a good friend for whom I cannot say too much.

ONLY PATROL ACTIVITY

From now (end of July) until the Battle of El Alamein, 'only patrol activity' figured almost daily in the Middle East communiqués. We often wondered whether the BBC announcer, whose familiar and well-modulated tones floated so incongruously over the arid wastes of scrub and gravel, had any idea of the laborious boredom these words described. It was routine work, intensely monotonous, which had to be carried out with a meticulousness that at times drove one to distraction. We had our fair share (and some more, we felt) and until well into September watched daily the slightest movements of enemy reconnaissance troops and OPs engaged on the same task as ourselves. Higher formations had apparently little to do save worry about the 'two met' (MT) that one had reported in the early morning. About midday, when the heat haze was so blinding that one could see nothing, frantic inquiries would come over the air, demanding the life history of these accursed vehicles. A couple of troops would eventually be put in motion to find them again and by the time that they had done so a message would come through to say that 'it doesn't matter now'.

At the start of these two months we formed part of a force called the 4th Light Armoured Brigade, earmarked to break through the enemy positions and carry out a harassing raid on his rear communications. Probably fortunately for us, this came to nothing and we reverted to 7th Armoured Division to function in the manner I have described, in the area bordering on the Qattara Depression and centring on a conspicuous hill called Himeimat.

There were constant advances and withdrawals of a mile or two each way, with the result that the ground became foul and infested with swarms of flies. Everyone acquired most unpleasant 'desert sores' and the majority had a bout of the malignant, though transient, sandfly fever. Poor Geoffrey Nares had the latter rather badly and was sent back to Cairo to recuperate. To our horror we heard that within a day of his arrival he had suddenly died, not of the fever but of what was subsequently found to be a tumour on the brain. It was a fearful tragedy – only a week before he had been among us, an enchanting personality and full of life and good spirits – and was made more so by its suddenness.

The mere fact that operations were of a static nature permitted a stream of visitors to come up and have a look round, either sightseers or newly arrived troops who wanted some experience. Quite a few of both varieties found their way to 'C' Squadron but of the latter I was blessed with Gerry Fuller and Valerian Wellesley. Gerry I had not seen for three or four years and we had much to discuss. Valerian graced our squadron for some time as he acted temporarily as second in command when Edward had to command another one. They were both in the Household Cavalry Regiment which, after many vicissitudes, had been finally converted into armoured cars. Their company certainly did something towards filling the gap left by Geoffrey's death.

The new army commander, General Montgomery, also came and had an informal look around wearing an Australian hat. He was very pleasant and was obviously taking pains to talk to and see the troops, an effort which his predecessor had apparently deemed unnecessary. SSM Ellen was still with the squadron and as he had originally been in the Royal Warwickshires, the general's old regiment, before coming to the 12th as band sergeant (he was a man of some versatility), he took up most of Monty's attention.

A special excitement had occurred a week or two previously when we had been astounded to hear that Winston Churchill was in the desert. A little later we were told that he was going to inspect representative units of the division, and I was sent off with seven or eight men to the rendezvous. It is not very easy to look smart after leading a John-the-Baptist-like existence for some months, but all the troops managed to beg or borrow clean and pressed clothes and I flatter myself that we looked tolerably presentable.

For an hour or two we waited on a dusty stretch of sand, but finally a cloud appeared on the horizon which became an immense cortège of staff cars, escorted by armoured cars on the ground and by fighters in the air.

We were all drawn up ready to receive the great man, flanked by a horde of press photographers with their cameras at the ready. Out of a milling mob of hangers on (never have I seen so many red hats in one place) emerged one central group, whose dominant figure could not be mistaken. I had seen him twice before, once at a ball at Blenheim where he lay on a sofa, his shirt ballooning, and discoursed to the French Ambassador, and once when he spoke to our division at Tidworth. But it had not struck me until now how small he was – not that an absence of inches mattered with someone of that personality. Clad in a siren suit, crowned with a topee of antique pattern (surely not the one he wore at Omdurman?), his face almost invisible for blue glasses and a fragrant cigar, he stepped busily along talking to Bill Carr.

He started speaking to the 11th Hussars in front of us; I strained my ears but could hear nothing save a sudden gurgle of rich laughter. I heard Bill saying my name and then my hand was being vigorously shaken.

'You're a very *young* man. How old are you?'

'Twenty-five, sir.'

'Well, well – and a major *and* you've got two of them.' He prodded vigorously at my medal ribbon. 'How splendid. But you look thin. Do you get enough to eat – and drink? Good, capital – and were you in France? Well, this is rather different, isn't it? – Well goodbye, my boy, and good luck to you.'

He moved on. I suddenly realised that something had gone wrong. In the excitement of the moment he had been led on past me and was now with the men behind instead of with my own people, who were standing rigidly, with moist palms and faces of anxious anticipation. It was too late. To our lasting regret he had passed on, beyond recall.

I was able to have a good look at the galaxy that followed. It included Montgomery, Alexander, Alan Brooke and Coningham – and most of them were covered with dust owing to having been put into an open car. Twenty minutes or so later the Prime Minister mounted his own car again and with a courtly wave of the topee drove on to see a squadron of his old regiment, the 4th Hussars.

On 28 August the Germans put in a heavy attack in an attempt to break the line and reach Alexandria. Their onslaught was quite expected and they achieved little save heavy losses. An enormous amount of their transport was lured into a shallow depression and was then most summararily dealt with, both by our guns and the RAF. My squadron was on the southern flank but we had little to do except in the initial stages when we watched the Germans endeavouring to penetrate the minefields, but they soon left this particular section and moved north. Neil, who was on my right, had a very busy time observing and locating the entire enemy advance under most adverse conditions. He did this with consummate success and subsequently received a very well earned MC.

A week or two after this abortive attempt we received our orders to return to the Delta to refit, with our own division, in preparation for the coming offensive, of which rumours were beginning to reach us. We went into camp at Khataba, just on the edge of the cultivation, and halfway between Cairo and Alexandria. The journey back was an eye-opener as we did nothing but pass endless, well-filled new aerodromes, vast tank and gun parks and camps full of troops. At last the tide of men and material had turned overwhelmingly in our favour.

The colonel sent everyone on leave as soon as possible, and Neil and I accordingly departed to Alexandria for an all too short holiday. The bathing was lovely and we spent most of our mornings on the beach. George Errington, an old friend, was about the place and through his kindness we were extended much hospitality, especially by Teddy and Nora Peel, in whose beautiful house and garden we spent many happy hours.

In the late afternoons we used to ride on Smooha racecourse and afterwards dine and wine at length, usually getting to bed nearer dawn than sunset. It was a complete break with the previous months and went far too quickly. Neil had an Alexandrian acquaintance who was almost pathetically anxious to provide diversion for us, and when at times his effusiveness became embarrassingly overwhelming we had to fabricate the most intricate alibis in order to escape his attentions.

When we returned to Khataba I discovered that I was to go

to Palestine, at once, on a three weeks' tactical course ('for prospective lieutenant-colonels') which had already started. Smallridge and I packed into a Jeep (I contrived to obtain a permit to take it to Palestine from Raymond Briggs, the new divisional commander) and drove to Gaza in a day – a most exhausting feat considering the heat crossing the Sinai desert.

At Gaza, which we reached late that night, I found a whole conglomeration of schools, all recently established. The course that I attended was really a glorified repetition of the one I had been to at Karkur in April, and some of the instructors were the same. It was fairly easy work, though there was a lot of new information about other arms to be acquired in a short time. There were some very good lecturers on the tactical side, and we were shown the exact method by which the Alamein line was subsequently forced. We had one or two very interesting talks from such varied experts as the Director of Military Intelligence, the head of the Middle East branch of the Ministry of Economic Warfare, and an eminent psychiatrist who told us of the rather alarming psychoses and complexes produced by long spells in the desert.

Each weekend I went to Jerusalem with Henry Howard (in the Coldstream) and we wandered around the Holy City, staying at the King David Hotel which was ruinously expensive and rather short of food. The only thing that marred our pilgrimages was that each weekend we succeeded in losing our way back to Gaza, on one occasion not returning until very late to find that a heavy storm had flattened the tents and scattered our belongings.

On my second visit to Jerusalem I spent a day with Mr Blatchford, the American vice-consul who was, I suppose, what would be called a Christian gentleman – to use an obsolete expression. He was a very old friend of my grandparents and had spent many years in Palestine looking after the interests of his countrymen, especially the YMCA. There was little he did not know of the politics and personalities of the country, and though he preserved an admirable diplomatic impartiality it was evident that his sympathies did not lie with the Jews. He showed me much of the city that I would not have been likely to have seen in other circumstances, as he had the entreé into the most closely guarded sanctuaries. I was deeply impressed by the Church of St Marie Réparatrice where beyond a magnificent iron grille the nuns in their blue and white habits prayed (in relays) for the sins of the world. In spite of their almost total enforced seclusion, Mr Blatchford, as a person of proven rectitude and advancing age, was allowed by the Mother Superior to have a few minutes' conversation each week with an American nun of eighty.

He gave me luncheon in his attractive house and I stayed a long time talking of my family. I had lived so long among soldiers, always in the immediate present, that it was a relief to come into the tranquil company of one who had time for a detached view of life and still saw a lot of good in man. I and my contemporaries were perhaps inclined to see the termination of the war as the gateway to a golden future. To Blatchford, for all its effects, good and bad, the war was nothing more than another seething in the perpetual brew of history. He attributed to man far less power to rehabilitate the world than we were all so confidently taking on trust. Though I saw the force of his reasoning, I could not quite believe in it then, though now I have come to agree with it fully.

I hated having to leave him, to return to a world which was pulsing too fast, but I felt serener for a few hours of his companionship. He loaded me with presents – Chesterfield cigarettes (a rare luxury), some wine and his own copy of Browning – and I returned to Gaza to study the best way of forcing a minefield.

The course ended without discredit befalling me and, bidding farewell to Henry, bound for Syria (how I envied him), I once more crossed the Sinai Desert. I stopped one night in Cairo and discovered that the regiment was bivouacked on the main Alexandria road, in a state of immediate readiness to move. Edward had organised everything to perfection in my absence. I was immediately plunged into a long series of conferences to study the coming battle.

ALAMEIN

By October 1942 the 8th Army was stronger than it had ever been before. Men and equipment had been arriving in increasing quantities and it was well provided with new Sherman tanks, 105 mm self-propelling guns, 6-pounder anti-tank guns and unlimited ammunition.

General Montgomery resolved his force into three corps – 10 (Herbert Lumsden), 13 (Lieutenant-General Horrocks) and 30 (Lieutenant-General Leese). 10 Corps contained 1st, and 10th Armoured Divisions and the New Zealand Division, and during the battle 7th Armoured Division came under command so that Herbert Lumsden was controlling an overwhelming force of armour, possibly 800 tanks. The Axis troops, on the other hand, had received hardly any reinforcements since their attack in August and still had only the two original Panzer divisions, 15th and 21st.

The plan envisaged an opening bombardment followed by an attack along the whole thirty-mile front, with two infantry attacks with special local objectives. These were to penetrate to the further side of the enemy minefields and there to establish two bridgeheads through which our armour would be passed when the Royal Engineers had cleared the way. The attack opened on 23 October and went more or less according to plan except that it took rather longer than was anticipated. The Germans so effectively covered the bridgeheads with batteries of 88 mm anti-tank guns that our own armour was temporarily neutralised and it was not until these formidable obstacles were liquidated by further infantry night attacks that we could finally advance.

It can be appreciated that the staff work to regulate the massive columns of tanks and vehicles through the different sets of minefields was Herculean. The whole enterprise was admirably coordinated, with the result that units arrived at their positions with the punctuality of express trains. It had all been carefully rehearsed in the desert, east of the Cairo-Alexandria road, and its efficiency bore witness to much patient practice and far-sighted planning.

We ourselves, like most other armoured car regiments, were to move up behind the tanks and slip through behind the enemy when the chance offered, to do as much damage as we could to transport. The Royals were actually the only regiment able to do this and managed to cause considerable havoc in the rear of an already demoralised enemy. When our division did break through it was pushed on at such a rate that we had to be used for our ordinary role of advanced reconnaissance.

On 20 October we began moving up towards the battle area. There were vehicles and guns everywhere and there was no doubt of the magnitude of the impending attack. On the night of the 23rd we heard the initial bombardment of 800 guns, and a little later began our move, ending up in the middle of our own minefields. Here we hung about for a day or two while the battle raged for the bridgeheads. At this time the German artillery was still functioning to some advantage.

In the ensuing days we continued up the minefield roads in the wake of our tanks but still had nothing very much to do. We were able to see a great deal of the battle and as we were on the 'main' road we heard all the latest news. Herbert Lumsden I saw several times on a General Grant tank tearing up to the fighting but finding time to wave his hand to us. The army commander also passed us and this probably gave rise to a completely unauthenticated rumour that 'WC' was demanding why the battle was not progressing much faster In fact the decisive armoured battle began on 1 November and from then everything went well. Enormous numbers of prisoners started walking in, and we ourselves were kept very busy extracting them from pockets which were laid bare by the gradual advance. Our bombers filled the sky; I had never seen anything like it.

On the night of 2/3 November we got our orders to follow the enemy who was now retreating in some hurry. By dawn we were pushing through the last confusion of minefields and the scene of the recent struggle, a grim and battered stretch of desert, littered with burnt out tanks and dead bodies. Enemy shelling had almost ceased, but Mark Wyndham's car was blown up by a mine. Luckily no one was hurt.

My squadron was first turned up northward to cut off anything that might still be on the coast road, but there were still a few rearguard troops who kept us off. On the 5th we turned westwards again and began to move faster down, and on each side of, the coast road. Hidden mines were a particularly unpleasant hazard and I lost three cars. The mines usually blew off one wheel and stub axle without injuring any personnel. Our excellent LAD was not far behind, and by dint of hard work and cannibalising good parts of a dismembered vehicle to repair another they managed to return me two cars within twenty-four hours, despite the fact that I was moving ahead steadily.

In the late afternoon we reached Daba, which was full of surrendering Italians whom we sent marching down the road to captivity in good order. The RAF were anxious to get the landing ground here into working order for their fighters as soon as possible and it says much for the general planning of the advance that as we were leaving the village at one end, a long convoy of RAF ground staff lorries was arriving at the other.

Shortly before dark we received orders to rendezvous with the rest of the regiment on the railway line. Here we found most of the division concentrated, with everyone busy filling up their vehicles. I found the colonel, very busy and surrounded by maps, who said that the whole division was going to move in a solid body to Kalda, south of Matruh, with the intention of turning north to Matruh if there was any likelihood of cutting off large enemy forces there. I had to send out three troops ahead of the main body.

It was a very dark night and exceedingly difficult to keep contact with the vehicle in front. This was made no easier by the towering clouds of dust churned up by the heavy Grant and Sherman tanks. SSM Robinson was in a Jeep and managed to keep us all together by the most prodigious exertions. RHQ, who were just in front of us, contrived to go off at a tangent and had a very adventurous night, including some indecisive skirmishing with isolated enemy pockets.

I know of nothing more diabolical than driving at night over bad going, hermetically sealed within an armoured car so that the light may be turned on, and wrestling with vagrant maps and the wireless. Sergeant Francis, my operator, was a man in a thousand, who could be relied upon to retain his sang-froid indefinitely – mine usually dissolved after an hour – and was an absolute wizard on the wireless. He could always accurately read speech when, to me, the machine was emitting a succession of noises like the Last Trump. After dark the wireless was almost invariably jammed by other stations, made worse by atmospherics. One could spend half a night trying to receive an important message from a troop and just miss its meaning. Nothing could be more tiring to both parties.

When it became light we were still some miles from Kalda. The division looked vast and inexorable, 2,000 vehicles or so moving in open formation. RHQ were still having their own troubles so I sped on and saw Roger Peake, the GSO1, rambling along in his armoured command vehicle – an enormous steel-plated office for seven people on a London omnibus chassis. He told me to slip on ahead. This we did, after a stolen halt for breakfast.

An order of the day had said that El Alamein would 'make history' and we felt, with the enemy beaten, we really might be doing something towards ending the war. By 10 or 11 a.m. we had reached Kalda, where we met some of the 4th South African Armoured Car Regiment, who were also pushing ahead. Mine was the northernmost of our three squadrons and an hour or two later I received orders to go to Matruh. The RAF seemed to think it was only lightly held, and division wanted confirmation of this before advancing again.

Matruh one had to approach from the south or east, as coming in from the west entailed a long detour to avoid a deep wadi and minefields. Neil, who was further away, was going to try and do this, but it was obvious that I would be there before him.

At about 2 p.m. it started to rain. Rain is very rare in Libya and when it comes the heavens open. It made the going extremely difficult and we took a long time to cover the twenty or thirty miles to our objective. There was only one approach down the escarpment from the south; the eastern approach involved a long trek along the escarpment until one reached a descent to the coast road.

Michael Bradstock's troop became held up at the southern gate by enemy anti-tank guns and he had one car badly disabled. As soon as I reached him (by this time we were encumbered with eighty or a hundred prisoners) I saw we should have to take the eastern route, though I sent another troop (Leslie Munro-Hinds) to the west on the off chance of finding some kind of goat track into the town. Then, having collected the rest of the squadron, I started off along the escarpment with John Stimpson out in front. The rain stopped and it began to get dark and a slight mist arose. I was getting more anxious about reaching the road and getting rid of my prisoners than about reaching Matruh, as I was certain that there were only a few odds and ends there who would disappear that night.

Suddenly I saw a large concourse of vehicles coming towards me along the escarpment, a mile or so away. There was every reason to suppose they were British but I stopped and looked through my glasses, though visibility was becoming worse every minute. Still believing them to be ours, I moved on a little closer to see better, at the same time dispersing the squadron so that it would be ready to act in case they were not.

Some of them also came nearer and before I knew what had happened my own car was being heavily engaged with fire. Something like a whiplash stung my cheek, and Sergeant Francis beside me slumped to the bottom of the car with a large hole in his chest, killed instantly. I could hear all the other cars firing away hard. My mouth was full of blood but I managed to tell Corporal Plant, my imperturbable driver, to turn the car around. I also tried to talk on the wireless but it had become dislocated.

The car started to move but something hit it a tremendous blow, and I saw poor Plant subside over his wheel. A second later the car began to burn. Crawling forward I found that Plant was dead and I prepared to leave the vehicle. I got through the top, jumped down and sheltered under the leeward side. Firing was still going on around me and from the remander of the squadron.

I think I must have had a few minutes' blackout as I next remember Edward's car approaching, with him shouting 'Jump on'. I managed to clamber on and hung rather precariously onto his hand as we began to move. It was then that I was hit in the knee, and in the sudden shock I let go, although he tried to hold me. I do not remember hitting the ground. A buzz of German voices greeted my return to consciousness.

Suspension

A German NCO slapped a couple of field dressings onto my face and right leg and another man dumped me on the floor of a half-track troop carrier. By this time it was getting dark and my next recollection was of lying on a stretcher in a captured British ambulance.

A very gentle doctor re-dressed my leg and put something like a vast powder puff over my right eye and cheek, telling me not to remove it as he thought the eye might be injured. He followed this up with a powerful jab of something which rendered me oblivious of a night on the move. When I woke the following morning, the German group who had captured me had halted to brew up and generally sort themselves out. I felt quite awful physically and beset by an overwhelming despair. A draught of ersatz coffee, the first of many over the next two and a half years, did little to improve matters.

A colonel, I imagined Intelligence, came over to talk to me, a good-mannered, rather academic officer. Stupidly I thought he was bent on interrogation but then realised that he really wanted to chat. There was little he did not know and he was quite realistic about the war in North Africa being over. He said they were desperately strapped for petrol and every abandoned vehicle had to be ransacked in case it contained even a few litres. Their progress down the coast road would therefore be slow and with our preponderance of tanks and supplies he guessed that we would be moving rapidly south-westwards across the desert to Agheila or somewhere in that area to cut them off finally. This is what I thought as well. The situation was far from good, desperate in fact; even the Field-Marshal was worried. He pointed. 'He's just leaving us.' And there was Rommel, a distant figure in a long overcoat walking towards a light aeroplane which took off as soon as he was on board.

The colonel hoped my wounds would not turn out to be too serious. He had been in North Africa since the original German presence in early 1941 and seemed very familiar with the activities of our different armoured car regiments, particularly mentioning the 11th Hussars. To this day I do not know whether I was in Rommel's headquarters or in that of the Kiel group, a formation that had been well known in the desert for a long time. There were certainly a lot of senior officers about and there was that somewhat portentous atmosphere that usually hangs over higher formations in all armies.

Shortly afterwards this particular organisation got on the move, and I was escorted by an NCO with some German wounded to the verge of the coast road (down which we had travelled so euphorically in June) to await transport. This eventually appeared in the shape of a clapped out old lorry, into which we were bundled. By now I was wishing that liberating death would come, especially as my condition had brought on a severe attack of gyppy tummy, or something similar, which demanded frequent halts of the lorry. My fellow travellers, who were equally familiar with such symptoms, took a sympathetic view. One of them was kind enough to give me a slug of revivifying schnapps from his flask.

Quite apart from the fact that the left side of my mouth seemed to have extended itself by about an inch, the wound in my right leg was agonising and I thought I should probably lose an eye, I was suffering from appalling remorse. I realised what a mess I had made of the situation on the escarpment resulting in the deaths of Francis and Plant. They had both been with me for some months and we had lived intimately as one did in the desert. Obviously they had considerable trust in me, a trust that had been betrayed even if their deaths were blessedly instant. Plant was a piece of

English oak, a wonderful and patient driver. He did not care much for military responsibility, only accepting a corporal's stripes to enhance the dignity of the squadron leader. Some squadron leader. They are not forgotten by me.

I wondered what 'C' Squadron was up to; probably it was not far away. At least it was in good hands under Ned's courageous and competent leadership. He was to guide the squadron for the rest of the war, finally taking it into Venice. Meanwhile we endured a night at Tobruk in a sort of annexe to the hospital, under considerable bombardment from the air and tormented by mosquitoes. However, what little the Germans could do for their wounded they certainly did for me and I was treated with humanity and consideration.

The next morning, 8 November, before dawn, we were moved again in another decrepit lorry, but after a few miles this was stopped by the Feld Gendarmerie and commandeered for some more vital purpose. We were decanted onto the side of the road, still under the care of our NCO. There was a fair stream of somewhat disorganised traffic moving west, and with great enterprise he managed to insinuate his charges, two or three at a time, onto various vehicles but keeping me under his hand; not that I could have moved far, if minded to escape. At around midday he handed me over to the hospital in Derna, the little port that Philip Flower and I had visited so lightheartedly earlier in the year. Here the German medical officers were working swiftly in somewhat Hogarthian conditions. Casualties were lifted, if immobile, onto a table, examined and patched up if necessary while the doctor dictated a diagnosis to a phlegmatic NCO with a typewriter alongside. The emergent document, as in all armies, was at least in triplicate. One copy was pinned to the patient.

I came before an English speaker, extremely expert, who examined my eye with an old-fashioned magnifying glass and informed me that he did not think it injured but it would be X-rayed when I was evacuated to Europe. My knee, which looked worse than it was, was cleaned up and encased in some sort of rigid bandage. He told me that his forte was really plastic surgery and asked me to wait a little until the crowd had thinned; then he would sew up my mouth. Eventually I was pumped full of some local anaesthetic, which lasted for some hours, while he did a quite remarkable job. Little trace of the repairs remain and the corner of the lips only occasionally sags in times of fatigue or inebriation. Later on I was informed that the doctor – he bore a strong resemblance to Giscard D'Estaing – was an ace in this particular field, so I remain profoundly grateful to him.

An hour later I was sitting on a bollard in the late afternoon sun on the Derna quayside, awaiting my European passage and not presenting a very soldierly appearance. The right leg of my thin whipcord trousers was completely lacerated and bloodstained, and my shirt and khaki sweater were in no better shape. My cap had disappeared long ago, unable to be accommodated on the bandaged head, and my only tangible possessions were a wristwatch, a large penknife, a few hundred piastres and a wonderful coat bought at Cordings in London, made of sheepskin, covered with thin waterproofing. To this was pinned my ticket. The desert army was seldom smart but I was certainly less than smart; gone were the dreams of Count d'Orsay!

A large hospital ship lay in the harbour and wounded were being ferried out in lighters, their departure efficiently organised by a busy *feldwebel*. Eventually he indicated that I should embark but at this point he was stopped and given a sound cursing by a German major, perhaps thirty years of age, disporting one of the higher grades of the Iron Cross and the yellow cavalry shoulder badges worn by some of the Panzer Corps. Having reduced the NCO to pulp (though the man appeared to be doing his duty quite adequately) he informed me in good English that it would be better for me to travel in another vessel. He told me that he knew England well, that things were now very serious in North Africa, especially as the Allies had landed that day in the west. This was news indeed.

While we were having this encouraging conversation, the *feldwebel* (if anyone deserved a Ritterkreuz, he did) had filled up his lighter with wounded and was obviously awaiting my presence as I was shown on his manifest. He approached the major once again but on this occasion received such a broadside, probably including the threat of close arrest, that in saluting he nearly fell into the harbour. The major then told me that he was quite useless, 'a harbour pimp', and that he himself was arranging the embarkation of some of his own men on *that* ship, pointing to a vessel of singular elegance that I had not noticed before.

A young lieutenant with his arm in a sling now appeared with some twenty or thirty badly wounded men from the major's regiment who were assisted into another waiting lighter after the major had shaken them all by the hand. There was an emotional farewell to his subaltern who was given letters to take home and he then saluted me. I was hard put to return the compliment without a cap and probably resorted to that curious gesture beloved of American Presidents. He was obviously a fine soldier and I was much impressed by his solicitude for his men and for the wounded prisoner. He stood on the quayside until we were on our way, an impressive figure in the dying sun. The lieutenant, whose English was only a little better than my German, mentioned that he came from the Von Schlieffen family. He obviously hero-worshipped him.

Our lighter came alongside the graceful little hospital ship which I subsequently learned had been the Czar's Black Sea yacht before the First World War. Afterwards it had fallen into Greek hands and had been commandeered by the Germans in the Piraeus in 1941. The lieutenant took me under his wing and we shared a cabin, panelled, it was said, with every variety of Russian wood. He lent me some washing materials and I was able to clean myself up a bit, though unable to shave on account of the bandages. All the bathroom fittings bore the honoured name of Shanks & Co., Barrhead, Scotland, which took me back nostalgically to my grandfather's loo in his house in Kensington.

The German army doctor in charge of the ship was gloomy but relaxed. He paid me a visit as we moved out of the harbour with all our lights blazing, to give me some sleeping pills and the incidental information that his ship was frequently stopped by our destroyers. Whether it was searched on these occasions I could not find out, but decided to try to beat my sedation and keep awake, so that if any such intervention occurred I could hobble to the rail (our cabin was near the stern), drop into the sea and hope to be fished out by a British boathook. I was then extremely surprised to learn that we were going to Greece and not to Italy, which I had thought was always the destination of British prisoners of war. The lieutenant and I were given plates of hot noodles and some brandy and were not uncomfortable in our bunks. We landed at the Piraeus the following morning after an unmolested passage and that evening I was installed in the Sismanoglion hospital in Athens. This was a very modern building, seemingly largely of glass, efficiently administered by the Wehrmacht, with a highly competent medical staff assisted by Greek nurses. I lay in a ward with a difficult subaltern of a rifle regiment, a charming boy in the Gurkhas, barely out of school, and a vituperative Australian pilot, minus a leg. There were others but these I remember very well.

Physically I improved. My eye was found to be intact, my mouth healed up and I could eventually remove a singularly unattractive bristle of reddish beard to find that I had rather a nasty scar on one cheek. My knee and leg were said to be slower in improving but I was able to send a message to England through the Greek Red Cross (it lies before me as I write) allaying alarm and despondency at home, as I had been posted as missing.

The food was by no means bad, and we were given half a litre of retsina daily as well as a generous dollop of fiery Bulgarian brandy in the evening. This I found of enormous solace as gloom was inclined to coincide with sunset, and I used to think of that hour in the desert when usually the troops of armoured cars came in to leaguer at squadron headquarters for the night, and we used to have a dram or two of whisky, putting on our long sheepskin coats as the temperature dropped and the sun disappeared.

Within a day or two I fell into trouble quite undeservedly. All hospitals, especially military ones, have to endure a grand tour of inspection by the chief doctor and his myrmidons, but in this German one the progress became almost majestic. Never have I seen so many hangers-on as followed the Oberst Arzt. Teutonic discipline demanded that one should lie to attention, on one's back with the arms on top of the sheets. Unaware of this regulation I suppose I was in a more comfortable and dégagé attitude. Anyway, it was enough to unsettle the whole echelon. Notes were taken and a flush of excitement came to the cheeks of the ward sister, a lady of immense girth and stature.

That evening she arrived at my bedside with a reluctant Greek nurse propelling a trolley bearing all the paraphernalia of colonic irrigation. An enema adequate for an elephant, yards of rubber tubing and gallons of soapy water. I protested that I had no need of this service but the colonel had spoken and I was to reap the reward for my insolence. Schwester advanced with the nozzle while the Greek nurse slowly paid out a few fathoms of hose. Then, just before the critical moment, the sirens sounded, the lights went out and we were in for an air raid

Forgetting my splinted leg, I leapt out of bed, pursued by the sister with a spouting jet of water, the pressure of which would have played havoc with my poor intestines should 'completion' have been achieved. I managed to get behind the bed of the Australian pilot who, overjoyed with the situation, quoted ten to one against 'the old bitch' catching me 'with the bum gun'. I, meanwhile, pretended to feel faint and a sort of peace was patched up. The Greek nurse laughingly started to mop up a sea of soapsuds and the sister, who had technically carried out her orders, wrote to that effect in her report.

After a while life became tedious. Materially we were well looked after but my companions' conversation wore somewhat thin and there was practically nothing to read. The Greek nurses fed us snippets of news which they had picked up on the clandestine radio, a rather sad little orchestra sometimes played mournful tunes in the evening (luckily after brandy time), and we received visits from the Protecting Power acting for the Red Cross. Its Athenian representative was, I think, a Mexican consulate official, although what his own nationality was I had no idea. Polite but melancholy, he was invariably accompanied by his wife and daughter, neither remarkable for their beauty and always clad in fur coats and hats. They seldom spoke but the Australian pilot convinced himself that the daughter harboured a hidden passion for me. 'Just touch her up a bit, Pommy, and the Sheila's yours.' Quite how this seduction was to be managed, in public and under parental eyes, was not disclosed. The Mexican, for want of a better name, confined his conversation to me. It was limited but he liked to refer to the time when he had been in London (*'en poste'* would be too grand a term) and he and his family had much enjoyed their residence in Notting Hill Gate. I was able to tell him that my Great-Great-Aunt Fetty had lived at Hill Cottage in Aubrey Walk and that perhaps our paths had crossed. On the next visit these identical exchanges would occur again as I could not cajole him into other fields. Occasionally Madame would rapturously murmur 'Ah Notting Heel', and Mademoiselle would throw me one of her unsettling *oeillades*.

For some reason the consular party would only sit by my bed and I came to dread their visits. The Mexican himself really had precious little English or French. I kept asking him for books, but although assuring me that the Red Cross had a large library, he only produced a few copies of the *National Geographical Magazine,* some Italian journals about photography and one or two astonishingly pornographic novels in French, published I think somewhere in the Levant, which I declined to translate for the Australian.

After a month or more in hospital I gathered from the Mexican that we would all be departing by train very soon for Germany. He said he had permission to see us – sadly he would have to be alone – and would bring blankets and other comforts. The Australian's view on these may be imagined.

The day, or rather evening, of departure was not without emotion. The charming Greek nurses in our ward had somehow collected a basket of rather pathetic bits and pieces of food, which they could ill spare, and they all wept. I started to kiss them goodbye but this was stopped by the giant Schwester, to whom I gave the pornographic books in a parcel as a token of our appreciation. I think she thought it was chocolate. The German lieutenant with whom I had travelled from Derna came to say farewell and gave me some cartons of cigarettes (we all smoked heavily in those days). He was depressed: he had lost his arm and nothing would ever be the same as in the Afrika Corps. I had the impression he had no wish to return to Germany.

Finally some eight or nine of us were taken in ambulances to the railway station where an immensely long hospital train was waiting with steam up. We had been put into our allotted bunks in an overheated carriage when the Mexican arrived with bundles of beautiful thick brown blankets to add to our already oppressive bedclothes. He had also found a few more books. My share of the loot was a novel by Georges Bernanos, which I cannot recall, one or two flashy American gangster novels, and *The Pilgrim's Progress,* which I had studied, ad nauseam, at my private school and for which I had little affection. However, suitable gratitude was expressed, cordial handshakes were exchanged with messages to the wife and daughter, and with a final mention of Notting Hill Gate he was removed from the train and we set off for the Reich.

The Balkan part of the journey seemed interminable. It took the train three days to reach Salonika where more wounded were to be loaded. Thereafter our route was meant to go through Sofia and Belgrade and thence to Zagreb and Salzburg, but there were constant halts owing to partisan activity and frequent diversions had to be made down single lines. We discovered one morning that we had spent most of the night perched on a viaduct over a precipitous ravine, while the front part of the train was safely ensconced in a tunnel.

By this time it was midwinter, with snow lying everywhere; yet the internal heating enabled the orderlies to work in their shirt sleeves. A few Germans died, not of the heat but of their wounds, and their bodies were carried to the rear of the train where there was an unheated van used as a mortuary. The extremely bumptious *sanität* in charge of our carriage, who loved airing his English, told me that the system of distributing these corpses to their families on arrival in Germany was the most efficient in the world. There was no reason to disbelieve him. We were finally sent round almost to Budapest before getting on to more regular tracks into Austria. The combined effects of the *sanitat*'s political views, the tiresomeness of the officer of the rifle regiment ('It's our duty to escape'), the perpetual snowstorms, the lack of books and the fact that I had developed jaundice lowered me to an all-time nadir.

At Salzburg we had a long halt as many of the wounded were unloaded, including Jim, the Australian aviator, whose stump was giving trouble. It was sad to see him go; his pungent views on life had done much to keep up our spirits and I only hoped that he survived. During the wait the remaining patients were visited by *Mädchen in Uniform*, a not very prepossessing collection of girls who distributed favours to the wounded – not their own, but cigarettes and small quantities of lethal-looking sweets. As soon as they reached our carriage they assumed expressions of dislike and closed their haversacks. I was doubly sorry that Jim had left us.

One vignette remains in my memory of Salzburg. On the opposite platform a few people were awaiting an incoming train, amongst them a very distinguished-looking man in a long smart overcoat with a fur collar. He was accompanied by a beautiful lady, presumably his wife, and, presumably also, their two sons. The elder, on crutches, had probably been discharged from the Army, his face still a mass of scars. The younger, a cadet, looked no more than sixteen and both he and his mother were unable stop their tears. The sight of our train full of the detritus of war cannot have helped. They looked delightful, civilised people and I pray that the poor boy did not end up in Russia.

A reduced hospital train took us at a greatly increased speed through Germany. National pride was focused on the railway system, with engines all painted with the slogan 'Räder müssen rollen für den Sieg'.* German railway officials enjoyed an authority and status that has not been seen in Britain since nationalisation. In all too short a time, by which I was fairly yellow with my disease, we arrived at the Prussian city of Magdeburg. Owing to some administrative hitch we were left on the platform like orphans of the storm, strapped in our stretchers and covered only by a sort of groundsheet which slowly accumulated the drifting snow. An exceedingly unpleasant and probably incompetent NCO appeared with a millboard, obviously having mislaid us and having received an appropriate cursing. Fortunately he could take it out on some underlings as we were bundled into the back of an ancient lorry. My stretcher was tipped up at forty-five degrees so that the blood drained into my head. I

* 'Wheels must roll for victory.'

managed to make enough noise to have the lorry stopped and the stretcher realigned before we lurched through a succession of grim streets to land up at the portals of what looked like a music hall.

Its palmy days were probably some half a century earlier and even then the clientele would have been seedy. In 1942 the auditorium was crammed with sick and dying Russian prisoners, hygiene was at a discount and the cynicism of the French doctors who were in charge of the inmates was not conducive to convalescence. Five or six of us were lodged on the first floor in a sort of *salon privé* with a window which looked onto the main part of the theatre and the stage, both of which were packed with rows of our unfortunate allies. Our rations were meagre enough, but theirs seemed to be practically non-existent apart from a desperate form of soup made from cabbage and potato peelings. The French doctors lived pretty well on parcels from home supplemented by black market additions. They were very ready to discuss gastronomic matters but in no way prepared to improve our diet. To add to our problems the whole place was infested with outsize bed bugs, swarming up and down the matchboard walls of our room when not sharing our blankets. The Gurkha officer, whose bed was by the inside window, reported that usually at least a dozen Russian corpses were removed each morning. Some rather macabre betting used to take place on the next day's score.

The subaltern from the rifle regiment, who could now walk, again raised the question of escape. His eyes had a strange look and I was convinced that he was all but insane. He announced to me one evening that he was 'going out' that night. I pointed out that it was snowing like mad, he had no overcoat, no German and no knowledge of the topography of Magdeburg. Where was he making for? He answered none of these questions. I could foresee a nasty situation: he would attempt to break out and we should all be punished as accomplices.

We were lucky. A call came for a volunteer to give blood for a transfusion for a British pilot shot down and lying in another hospital. The rifleman's group was the right one, so I ordered him into this humane task, telling him to use the opportunity to see what his chances were outside. As he had to walk a couple of miles each way through the snow, under armed guard, his enthusiasm cooled quite considerably and we were able to keep him tolerably quiet thereafter. Indeed he and the Gurkha, who were both mobile, soon preceded me to the prison camp, while I remained with the bed bugs and the dying Russians for a further week or two. I could eat nothing suitable for my jaundice, the wound in my leg declined to heal and the French doctors were kind enough to say that without reasonable food it never would. Finally I persuaded them to say that it was better than it was, and early in the new year I was despatched with an elderly guard to Spangenburg, near Kassel. The prospective delights of the Oflag were summed up by my escort as 'much food and much *füssball*'.

Spangenburg, a rather pretty little town, not far from Kassel, lay at the meeting of three valleys, surrounded by pine forest. It was dominated by an ancient and romantic-looking castle on a conical rock. This housed the Upper Camp, to which I was consigned, Oflag IX AH; the Lower Camp was just outside the town. Both were under the control of an elderly commandant, a retired cavalry officer, whom we hardly ever saw but who was found after the war to have acted very correctly, suppressing some of the more extravagant orders that emanated from the Führer's headquarters about the treatment of prisoners of war.

The walk from the station to the Kommandatur in the town and then up the hill, in snow and darkness, was testing. My right leg was really a passenger and I was unfeignedly glad to arrive at the portals of what looked like Castle Doubting in my recently discarded *Pilgrim's Progress*. Although it was better than that fastness, it was neither Shepheard's nor

Claridge's, but at least my reception was warming. Once through the guard room, where I was signed in and given a metal plaque numbered 1453 (easy to remember, the date of the Fall of Constantinople), I was in the hands of my countrymen. The adjutant, an equable and well-mannered Seaforth Highlander, and the doctor, Jimmy James, awaited me. The latter was quick to spot that I was in a decrepit condition and it was agreed that I should go at once into the sick bay and not be bothered by anyone. I did not then realise the insatiable curiosity (which I swiftly developed myself) that overcame all prisoners of war at the prospect of a new face with the possibility of fresh news.

The sick bay, empty at that time, lay in an isolated tower and here I convalesced very comfortably in welcome solitude. Jimmy James, a nice man and a very good doctor, especially in the psychological field, was obviously glad to have someone with a genuine wound rather than what he described as an unceasing procession of prisoners with piles and digestive troubles. My jaundice cleared up and I was spoiled by being given invalid food, something of a luxury in the camp. Books were brought to me and I had no visitors other than Colonel Henry Swinburn, in charge of security, who erroneously imagined that I might be the bearer of important messages from outside. A clever staff officer from the Indian Army, he had been G1 to the ill-fated Highland division at the St Valéry debacle in 1940 when General Victor Fortune was obliged to surrender. The latter, a great gentleman, was the senior officer in our rather elderly camp.

As soon as I was better, I had to go and give him an up-to-date account of outside hostilities as far as I knew about them. We covered the last year in North Africa and I rather put my foot in it by speaking unenthusiastically of Neil Ritchie, who for a time had commanded the 8th Army not very successfully. I did not then realise that he had been a brother officer (in the Black Watch) of the general, who was obviously much attached to him. However, being eminently fair, he took no umbrage and said that I should not conceal my opinions when I gave my 'lecture'. The prospect of this put me in something of a panic but I had been firmly told by Henry Swinburn and Ewan Miller (he had commanded the 60th Rifles at Calais and became a distinguished postwar general) that it was expected of me when I had recovered. Not only was I to prepare it for delivery as soon as possible but I must also have an alternative spoof one to be used should the German guards elect to appear. The subject of the latter was the flora and fauna of Lower Egypt with some observations on the seasonal rise and fall of the Nile. I reckoned on being able to waffle through this if necessary and I was promised that I would be asked questions to assist me. Sadly this pearl of topographical erudition went unrevealed as I had a 'goon'-free run for my peroration. Indeed the lecture, given to the entire camp, passed off rather well, especially as I had the advantage of knowing a little more than my listeners. Able hands drew maps and diagrams of North Africa on the blackboard, a mass of questions were asked and answered and, very temporarily, I was the man of the moment.

By this time I had emerged from the sick bay, feeling infinitely better and with the hole in my leg healing up, although the limb itself still looked like a matchstick. Jimmy James had looked after me very well and I had enjoyed being with him and his room-mate, the chaplain, an equally agreeable character, later to become the Dean of Peterborough. The chaplain had rather surprised me on the first morning by administering Holy Communion at the crack of dawn, before I could tell him that I had never been confirmed (one of my few acts of moral courage at Rugby), and before I could ask him if it was thought I was *in extremis*. My clothing had been removed and destroyed, with the exception of the beloved Cordings coat, and I was fitted out with various borrowed or donated garments as there was, as yet, no battledress of my size in the camp. A good Samaritan, Miles Reid, loaned me his second pair of trousers, a Christian gesture indeed.

I was now moved into the room high up in the castle which, with its seventeen other inhabitants, was to be my sleeping place for the next two years. We occupied double-decker beds with mattresses stuffed with straw and, as far as I can remember, an adequate amount of blankets. Certainly we were seldom cold in the winter; the castle was well heated by vast boilers in the dungeons, fired by wood which we used to cut during the summer in the forest. A strange figure presided over these lower regions called Kühlmer, who was apparently a permanent fixture in the castle. He paid not the slightest attention to either the British or the German guards and would have protracted shouting matches with both, always ending with the punchline that he recognised no military authority and was only answerable to his Führer and his God.

The senior officer in this room was Charles Newman, a building contractor in Essex before the war and a keen Territorial, and a quiet and much respected figure. He had found his way into the Commandos and in early 1942 led the very gallant and dangerous raid on St Nazaire for which he received the VC in 1945. Several of his officers had accompanied him to this camp and one of them, Ronnie Swayne, was to become and remain a close friend. An intellectual, a music lover and a dedicated fly fisherman, it seemed he might become a don. Instead he rose effortlessly in the shipping world to become head of Overseas Containers Ltd.

The castle housed something less than three hundred British officers and a number of other ranks who acted as orderlies. It was a fairly heterogeneous collection. A large number emanated from the 51st Highland Division, which in its revived form had arrived in North Africa before Alamein and was to cover itself with distinction in the remainder of the campaign there. Some of their regular officers, accustomed from an early age to generous daily measures of whisky, probably found their enforced deprivation something of a penance, which in some cases degenerated into withdrawal symptoms and an insensate desire for sugar.

There were some very agreeable people among them and I have pleasant recollections of my room-mate Rupert Christie, a major in the Gordon Highlanders. Intellectually well endowed, he possessed among many other accomplishments great fluency in Russian and a considerable knowledge of Russian literature. During this time there was much enthusiasm for all things to do with the Soviet Union and Rupert was persuaded to take classes of some of the younger officers who were interested in learning the language. He also gave talks on the great Russian writers. Becoming increasingly bored with the intensity and left-wing inclinations of his students, he finally decided to give a dissertation on two of the obscurer poets, Kalamatov and Katastrov, and was delighted when a lively discussion arose about the lives of these entirely fictitious characters.

Two inmates of Spangenburg were already well known to me. One was Wilfrid Davies of the 13th/18th Hussars, with whom I had been on a course – taken far too casually by me, with dire results – at Bovington in 1938. Cheerful and ebullient, he was a lover of gossip but seldom malicious. Nicknamed 'the Duck' on account of the rather curious action of his legs and feet, he was an entertaining companion. I had last seen him in the 1940 campaign.

The other was David Harrison, large, urbane and pink, a 4th Hussar captured in Greece. Living as he did for animals, he had never been militarily enthusiastic though he was always conscientious in the care of his men. Before the war he had lived in our mess at Aldershot when hunting the hounds there, a task which freed him from much irksome duty. A skilled breeder of foxhounds, he was to take on the South Pembrokeshire after the war, achieving many successes at Peterborough and elsewhere. In his latter years he came to live at Badminton and gave much assistance to 'Master' in the pursuit of perfection in this particular field. Although kind and easy to live with, he harboured a wholly unreasonable dislike of all the Scottish officers, in whom he could see no merit. He was very happy, on the other hand, to stand on the ramparts for hours, smoking his pipe and observing the many varieties of birds which flew around the schloss.

Miles Reid, whom I called the 'Lender of Heavenly Trousers', commanded the Phantom element in the lamentable Greek campaign. Originally a naval cadet (leaving the service through persistent seasickness), he had been a Sapper in the First World War, being both wounded and decorated. A good linguist, he had worked in one of the oil companies up to 1939, then returned to the army to serve in the Mission to the French in 1940 and after that with the Phantom. Although a certain age and with two sons in the Army, he had been dispatched with his squadron to Greece, although he had some rather sardonic remarks to make about his selection in preference to younger men. He had had a very rough time there before eventual incarceration. About his adventures, which ended in Colditz, he wrote modestly and well after the war. Intelligent and witty, he remained a friend to me and all my family for the rest of his long life.

Another redoubtable character was Jack Poole. A young officer in the previous war in the 60th Rifles he had been taken prisoner early on, only escaping towards its end. Thereafter he had served in the Sudan Civil Service, returning to the 60th in time to be taken prisoner for the second time at Calais. By the end of hostilities he had had nearly a decade in all in durance saying that on the whole it had been no worse than his time at Rugby. We had a strong bond over our dislike over that establishment and I am afraid declined to join the other Rugbeians in the camp, who wanted to waste a precious letter form (only two allowed each month per officer) to the Headmaster saying that we were in good heart. Jack did add on second thoughts that perhaps we owed the place some gratitude in preparing us for the bloodiness of

Spangenburg. A great stoic, he suffered many troubles after the war but was never known to complain.

I cannot say that I was ever able to arouse much enthusiasm for the possibility of escape. Indeed the whole thing filled me with apprehension, as so many better qualified people than myself had failed so abysmally in their attempts to get out. It was a relief when some time in 1943 we received a message through the illicit radio from General Eisenhower absolving officers in prison from this duty owing to the unlikelihood of the Germans continuing to respect the civilised rules of war.

One or two people had, or had almost, got out of Spangenburg disguised as German officers and there had been an inventive plan to swing a boom across the dry moat which encircled us in the few minutes when the sentries' attentions could be diverted. For some reason this had come to naught. A wild-eyed Northumbrian, too, had tried to enlist my services in digging a vertical shaft down through the floor of a storeroom. This would have to descend through solid rock for some unbelievable distance until it was below the level of the dry moat, when a tunnel would be made at right angles to emerge on the naked glacis of the castle mount. It seemed rather a long-term policy but no doubt kept its participants out of mischief. Luckily I was able to plead my leg and when it had healed I was in the position of being able to whisper the magic word 'Security', which admitted of no inquiries. 'Security' was really too grand a term for the activity in which I was to become engaged, which was in fact to do with the dissemination of news. The camp was seldom without some kind of radio receiver, and although periodic German raids tended to locate and destroy the current model, it was always rapidly replaced by the ingenuity of two or three experts, the leader of whom was the proprietor of a fly-tying business in Inverness and possessed of remarkable skills with his fingers.

Reception tended to be muted so that half a dozen of us sat

round the set, each writing down in a sort of shorthand a particular portion of the BBC news. We then pooled our results and, under an editor, managed to produce a bulletin, most evenings, to be read in the various rooms when immunity from prying Germans was assured by stooges placed at strategic points. All this took quite a long time and was quite rewarding, although it did not inspire me towards journalism. The news team had an additional task in the shape of security messages that came in code through certain broadcasts (notably those of the Radio Parson who must have had his homilies severely doctored). These all had to be passed on to Henry Swinburn, nicknamed 'the Filter'.

In addition I undertook the onerous task of laundry officer for my room, apparently showing such expertise in this field that I was promoted to second-in-command of camp laundry, a post which enabled me to have certain contacts with the Lower Camp. These were particularly useful when either of the two establishments was temporarily bereft of its wireless sets. The washing of our clothes was all done under contract with a laundry in the town, and by judicious bribery with soap and cigarettes (of which we had ample supplies,) much useful information and occasionally food could be obtained from the guards and *blanchisseuses*.

The former were mostly elderly soldiers who had fought in the previous war and only wanted a quiet life and the avoidance of being sent to the Russian front. The security personnel were largely schoolteachers or other academics with good English. The chief of them, Hauptmann Seybold, was not without humour and prided himself on his knowledge of the idiomatic use of our tongue. He was reputed to be the originator of the classic saying, after a satisfactory morning's search for a radio, 'You British think that I know fuck nothing, I tell you that I know fuck all.'

I felt guilty at times that I did not throw myself more into some specific study either of languages or of recondite subjects like economics or political theory, but both enthusiasm and application were lacking. However, thanks to a very adequate library I did settle down to reading for several hours a day, mostly history and biography and memoirs as well as the great Victorian authors, notably Thackeray and Trollope to whom I have remained loyal all my life, though owing to some quirk of nature I have never been able to get on terms with Dickens.

Books did eventually arrive from England and I was grateful to the excellent Mr Francis whose shop at the Piccadilly end of Princes' Arcade I had long patronised. He despatched me a parcel every month, well chosen and varied and of a nature not needing heavy German censorship. We all gave our volumes, when read, to the library which built up to quite substantial proportions over the years. It was wonderfully organised and catalogued by Charles Shears, an erudite and delightful publisher, of whose company many of us were very fond. So much so that we composed a sort of anthology in his honour, of original pieces. I have a faint idea that I wrote a learned paper on early English explorers, Sir John Mandeville and so on. Charles managed to get this back to England and had it bound and I wonder what happened to it after his death.

The German provision of food was ungenerous although the black bread, if rank in flavour, was at least filling. Sauerkraut and other cabbage derivatives played a large part in the rations, though personally I had the strongest aversion to these vegetable delicacies and still have. Each prisoner was supposed to receive a Red Cross parcel weekly containing various bits and pieces of tinned food, coming into Germany through Switzerland. But with increasing disruption of the railway system through bombing, the delivery of these became somewhat spasmodic although the British officers in charge of our commissariat had prudently built up some reserves. Even so, these were seriously eroded by the end of the war.

The Red Cross parcels were treated as rations and distributed as such to each mess of six or eight officers, but some of us were lucky enough to have extra gifts of food from sources in North and South America and elsewhere. I was very touched to receive some parcels from my friend Michael Grissell, incarcerated since 1940 in another camp and well supplied through American contacts of his mother. And also from a completely unknown Dutch butcher in the town of Waalwijk who must somehow have learnt of my name. Holland was desperately short of food and it seemed remarkably generous and self-sacrificing to send me tins of meat and apples. After the war, by devious means, I was able to send the Dutch butcher two new bicycle tyres which were, I was told, more prized there than anything else.

Our mess, which included David Harrison, was well managed by Bob Windus, a colonial servant from Cyprus, and we fared probably somewhat better than most people. Bob was a good German speaker and had one or two useful sources of supply through the guards, one of whom he discovered to be a fellow Freemason.

Sometime in the winter of 1944-45, when we were on very short commons, it was announced that a long-awaited consignment of Red Cross parcels had arrived at the station. Our British orderlies were sent off with the much-used handcart (employed in laundry activities and once figuring in a drama of attempted escape) which finally returned bearing a heavy crate lavishly labelled with red crosses and the insignia of St John. Opened with ceremony at the commissariat it was found to contain nothing but a set of curling stones, 'stanes' in the vernacular, sent from wellwishers to the officers of the Highland Division who were anxious to pursue their national sport on German ice in the moat. The vituperation that ensued, particularly that of David Harrison, lay heavily on the heads of the Scots who were obliged, thereafter, to play their curious game rather more furtively – and on continuing empty stomachs.

A low diet did not foster too much energy but the games-mad were able to play cricket, hockey and football of a sort in the moat. Some desultory gardening also took place and by giving one's parole (surrendering to the guardroom one's identity plaque) it was possible once or twice a week to leave the castle on an organised walk. In summer, longer outings took us to the surrounding woods where we cut up timber for the voracious central heating furnace. I found these expeditions not disagreeable and they certainly helped, temporarily, to dispel claustrophobia.

People were always ready to lecture on various subjects, not all of them very rewarding. There was almost invariably someone who had some knowledge of such diverse matters as the Albigensian Heresy, the classified claret growths of Bordeaux, the manufacture of scent, the breeding of racing pigeons, heraldry, the Pentateuch and so on. But the arts certainly flourished as there was a proliferation of painters. An orchestra, musical appreciation and the use of instruments all lay under the benign direction of the gifted Donald Frazer who had been commanding the 15th/19th Hussars in 1940 when I had last seen him. I believe also that there were one or two sets of bagpipes but their use was actively discouraged. George Lascelles, now Lord Harewood, had come to the camp in 1944 after being wounded in Italy, and began, before being removed to Colditz, his intense study of musicology which has since paid such dividends.

The drama prospered and by the end of our time remarkable productions were being mounted, a vast improvement on the extremely amateur ones into which I had foolishly been inveigled earlier. In one of these, a Ben Travers farce, the highlight was a major row between one of the actors and the prompter, accused, not without reason, of being asleep.

Letters from home were very much the lynchpins of our existence and the arrival of the post, at irregular intervals, never failed in its excitement. I still recall the thrill, some weeks after my coming into the camp, when someone appeared in the library to tell me that there were a dozen letters awaiting me on my bed. To later generations it is hard to understand the emphasis, particularly in wartime, that was put on the amenity of correspondence, not to mention the art of précis-writing imposed by the limits of letter cards and sheets of prescribed lengths. People in England were incredibly considerate and consistent about this and I remain eternally grateful to my many correspondents, family and otherwise, and especially to Ursula Wyndham, whose letters I wish I could have preserved as they were models of wit, interest and style.

News filtered in of the 12th Lancers and I was able to obtain a fair idea of where everyone was and what had happened to them. After completing the North African campaign in May 1943 the regiment was in Algiers for some months before embarking for Italy, there enduring an unpleasant and largely static winter campaign when at times it had to act as infantry. But it ended the war in a blaze of glory and excitement when, in its true armoured car role, it was pushed far ahead of the 8th Army, now commanded by Dick McCreery, to liberate and occupy Venice and Trieste in the spring of 1945. Most of my friends and companions were still there, though George Kidston, who had done outstandingly well, had been invalided home after the German defeat in Tunisia, to be succeeded as colonel by Kate Savill who commanded with equal panache until the end of the war. Tim Bishop, too, had been invalided home and had found himself a bride.

Sometime in January 1945 I heard with shock on the BBC news that Herbert Lumsden had been killed in the Far East by a kamikaze pilot on Admiral Fraser's flagship. After Alamein he had fallen out, not for the first time, with Monty over the question of cutting off the retreating German troops, as anticipated by the intelligence officer to whom I had talked. Summarily sent home, he appears to have been sympathetically received by Winston Churchill who despatched him to General MacArthur as his special representative. No doubt he carried out this task with his usual flair but I was only one insignificant person among hundreds of others more important and qualified who were unanimous in regretting that such talent should have been confined to such an inactive role. Personally I felt his loss very keenly; his example had meant much to me, as it did to all who served with him in France and the Middle East.

Although Arnhem had proved so gallantly disastrous (it provided us with a further influx of prisoners) and the Ardennes offensive had shown that there was still some German strategic punch, the Allied advance was in full flood. Towards the end of March it was apparent that the American 2nd Army was advancing rapidly eastwards and should reach us within weeks or even days. The Germans let it be known that they were under orders to move us out of the camp and we prepared ourselves. Charles Newman, who was in charge of the kitchens, managed to load a certain amount of food and cooking material onto the famous handcart and a second one was produced for the doctor's stores. By this time many of the older prisoners were in a weak condition and it was obvious that a forced march would produce its casualties, especially as most of us were carrying thirty pounds extra of belongings and food.

On 30 March we finally moved out of the castle sometime in the afternoon, accompanied by our guards and the whole of the Kommandatur staff-interpreters, censors and so on. Although few of us were in much shape physicallly everyone was in the highest spirits knowing that the American troops were not far away and we were in sound of perpetual gunfire. The secret wireless, the 'canary' as it was called, had to be dismantled before we set out, so exact news was not readily to hand.

As far as I can recall we marched during two nights, lying up each day in farm buildings in different villages, watching the retreat of the varied elements of the German army and its enforced allies. I suppose we had covered some thirty miles eastward from Spangenburg when we reached a considerable river, the Wehra, which some of us thought might temporarily delay the American advance. During the night march, I and one or two others managed to remove ourselves from the column – not a very difficult operation as the guards were elderly and tired.

With Ronnie Swayne, a very good companion in such an adventure, and one or two more we endured two further days and nights of acute discomfort in the surrounding woods. Early April rain was heavy, cold and infinitely wetting and there was an unpleasant eerie feeling in the seemingly empty countryside with shells passing overhead. In fact there were little groups of escaped prisoners and refugees all over the place, as well as bodies of armed Hitler Jugend, hair-triggered adolescents to be avoided at all costs.

We established ourselves in quite a good position of observation and were finally able to see American troops crossing the valley beneath us. Not all were immediately friendly at being greeted by a group of sodden ragamuffins. I remember being rather shocked at the amount of rings they had on their fingers, presumably looted.

Rapport was finally established and after some delay we were despatched in a lorry to the local town of Eshwege and handed over to a workshop detachment of the American Army, who were using the deserted airfield to repair vehicles. Their personnel were veritable Vulcans and worked day and night mending tanks and lorries which had broken down in the headlong advance. Their commanding officer loaded us with food and then gave us – we were perhaps twenty strong by now – ancient French rifles and cartridges, asking us to guard the airfield perimeter against stray Germans, as he had no troops to spare. We organised ourselves into shifts, periods of patrolling interspaced with rest in the not very luxurious barracks. Luckily our military prowess was not called upon.

In the end most of the original inhabitants of the camp

arrived in dribs and drabs, and certain senior officers began flexing their muscles. By now the airfield was being used by American Dakotas flying in petrol for the advancing forces and it was arranged that we should be taken to their base at Luxembourg in the empty returning planes.

It was a memorably cold flight as to facilitate the swift unloading of the fuel drums the rear doors had been removed and we were subjected to an icy draught as we lay huddled on the floor. Fortunately some of us had equipped ourselves with German parachutists' smocks which were very warm and had fur-lined hoods. The pilot and his loaders were none too happy about some odd German fighters said to be on suicide missions, so that it was a relief to touch down in the Grand Duchy. Here we were speedily entrained the same day for Paris and were ensconced that night, after a reasonable supper, in the Hôtel Scribe. It was an uncanny joy to have a room to one's self, to have a bath and the luxury of sleeping in sheets.

We were now in the hands of the British and the next morning were subjected to 'de-briefing'. Why we were required to fill in interminable questionnaires and be interviewed by a large staff of young men and women (who one thought could have been actively employed elsewhere) Heaven alone knows, and I fear they received some rather dusty answers. No one was supposed to leave the hotel until everyone had been through this process but I could not resist walking out into the Rue Scribe. Paris was looking exactly as it should on a spring day.

A sort of military Cerberus guarded the doors and while I was remonstrating with him saying tht I only wished to go out onto the pavement, a vision of feminine charm and elegance, dressed in a uniform obviously made by Paquin or Lanvin, floated in to inquire whether any of the returning prisoners would like a drive round the boulevards. It was the beautiful Lady Orr-Lewis, last seen in Cannes five years ago. Thanks to her and her companions we were cosseted and pampered until such time as we were to be flown to England in the late afternoon, and around six we reached Wing near Aylesbury.

The not unfamiliar treatment of tea and sympathy brought me finally home.

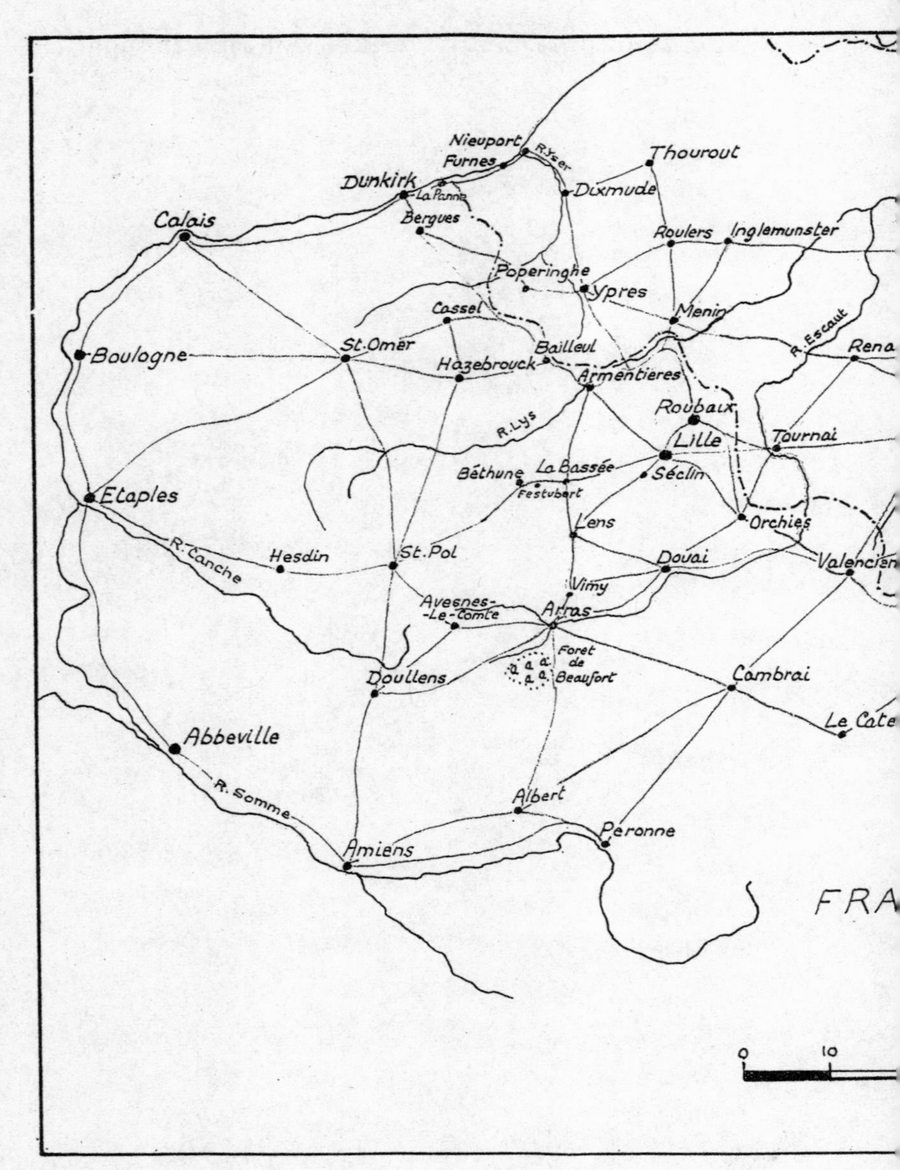
THE X.
Northern
Nieuport
R.Yser
Furnes
Thourout
Dunkirk
La Panne
Dixmude
Calais
Bergues
Roulers
Inglemunster
Poperinghe
Ypres
Cassel
Menin
R. Escaut
Boulogne
St.Omer
Bailleul
Hazebrouck
Armentieres
Rena
R.Lys
Roubaix
Lille
Tournai
Béthune
La Bassée
Séclin
Festubert
Etaples
Lens
Orchies
R. Canche
Hesdin
St.Pol
Douai
Valencien
Vimy
Avesnes-
-Le-Comte
Arras
Foret
de
Beaufort
Doullens
Cambrai
Le Cate
Abbeville
R. Somme
Albert
Peronne
Amiens
FRA
0
10

)LANCERS.

nd Flanders.

940.

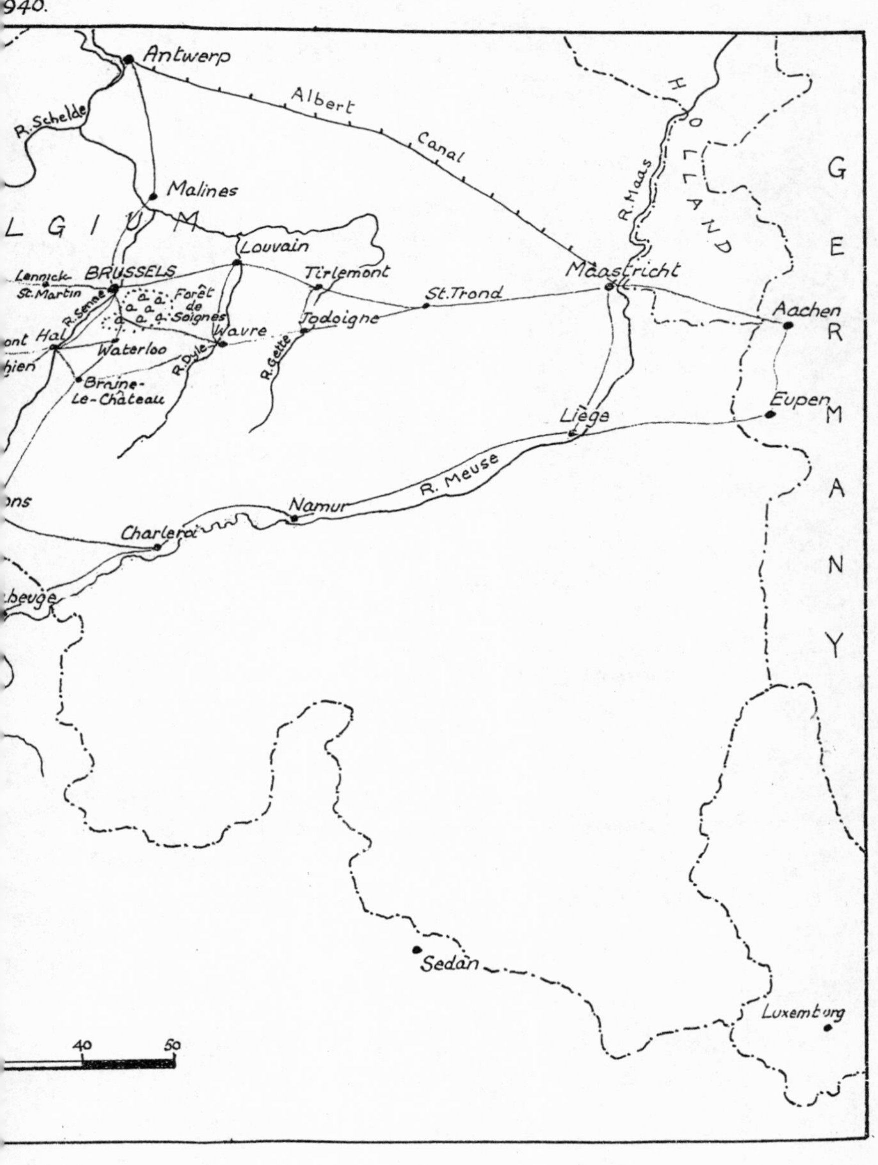

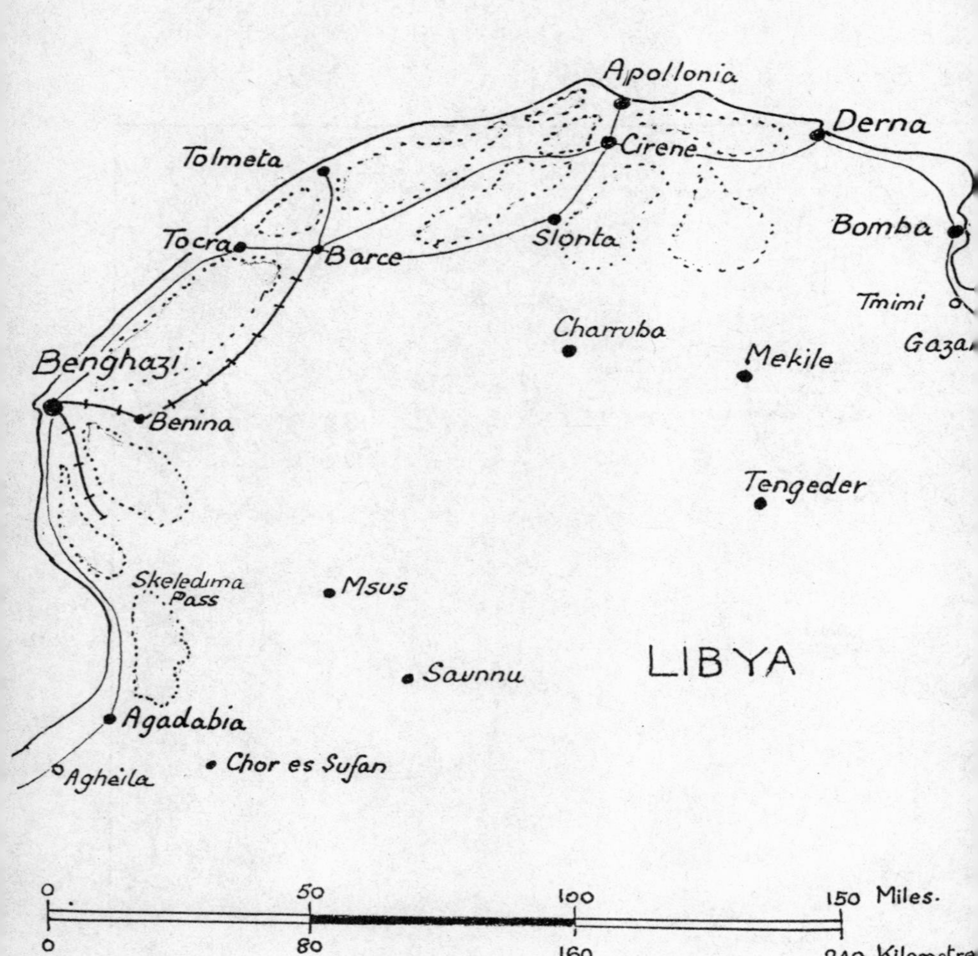
Apollonia
Derna
Cirene
Tolmeta
Bomba
Tocra
Barce
Slonta
Tmimi
Charruba
Gaza
Mekile
Benghazi
Benina
Tengeder
Skeledima
Pass
Msus
LIBYA
Saunnu
Agadabia
Chor es Sufan
Agheila
0
50
100
150 Miles
0
80
160
240 Kilometre

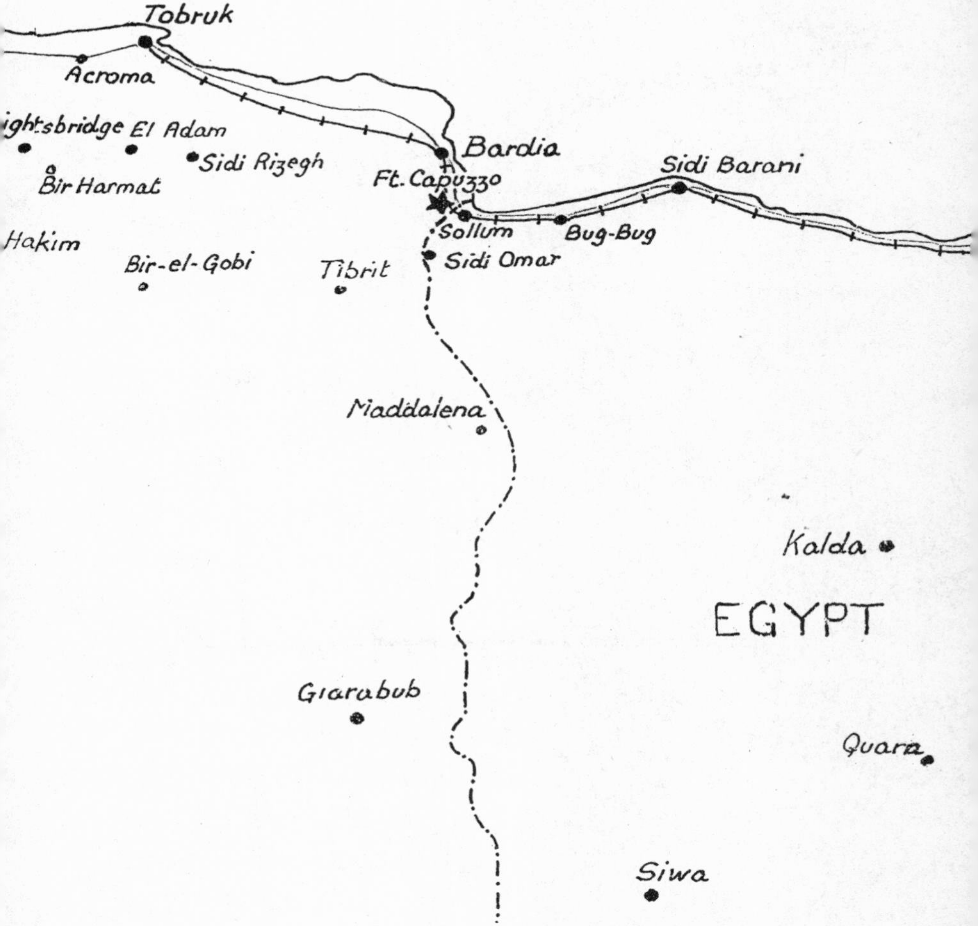

Tobruk
Acroma
ightsbridge
El Adam
Sidi Rizegh
Bir Harmat
Hakim
Bir-el-Gobi
Tibrit
Bardia
Ft. Capuzzo
Sollum
Sidi Omar
Bug-Bug
Sidi Barani
Maddalena
Kalda
EGYPT
Giarabub
Quara
Siwa

continued overleaf

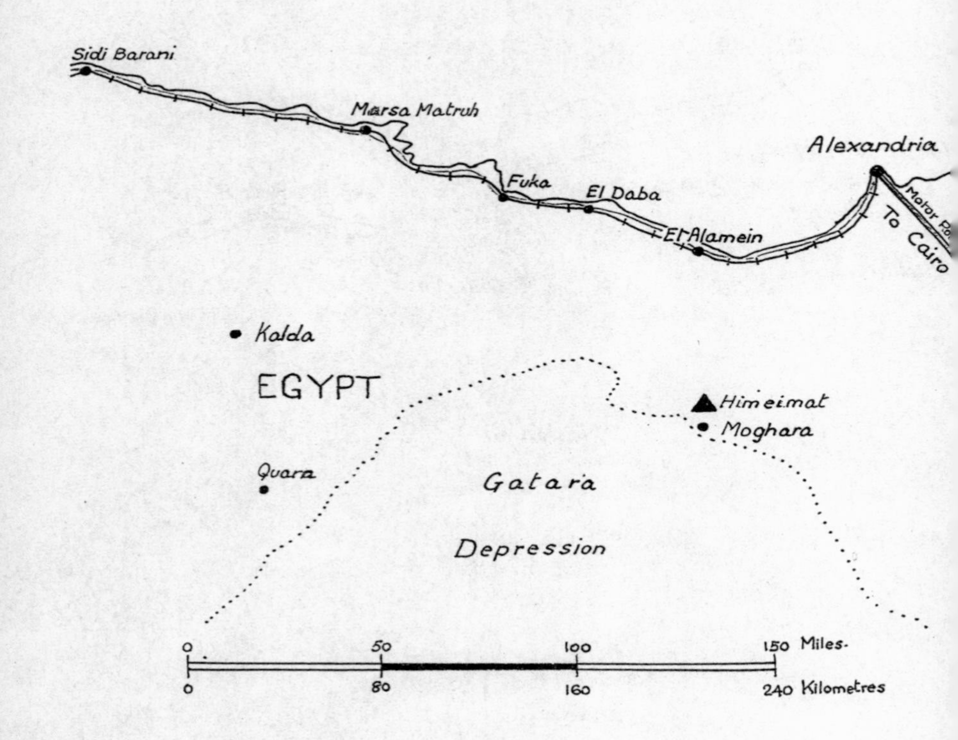
Sidi Barani
Marsa Matruh
Alexandria
Fuka
El Daba
El Alamein
Motor Ro
To Cairo
Kalda
EGYPT
Himeimat
Moghara
Quara
Gatara
Depression
0
50
100
150 Miles.
0
80
160
240 Kilometres

Index

Abraham, Matt, 69
Alanbrooke, Field-Marshal Lord, 62, 78, 79, 130
Alexander, Field-Marshal Lord, 58, 62, 130
Amaklavari, Colonel, 107-8
Arkwright, Frank, 15, 126
Arkwright, Peter, 36, 46, 52, 53, 54
Arlen, Michael, 76
Auchinleck, Field-Marshal Sir Claude, 77-8

Baddeley, Hermione, 72
Bailey, Percy, 22
Bailey, Tim, 22
Baring, Esmond, 117, 118
Barker, Maurice, 66, 79, 87, 88, 89
Batchelor-Taylor, Adrian, 70, 75
Beaverbrook, Lord, 65
Bennett, Constance, 26
Bishop, Tim, 36, 37, 38, 42, 48, 49, 50, 60, 72, 73, 86, 163
Blakiston-Houston, Major-General M., 16
Blatchford, Edward, 132-3
Bradstock, Michael, 138
Briggs, Major-General R., 132
Brinton, Tatton, 39
Brookbank, Robin, 126
Brooke, Alan, *see* Alanbrooke
Brooks, Teddy, 18
Browne-Clayton, William, 38, 69, 79
Browning, Lieut-General Sir Frederick, 75
Burne, Peter, 79, 84, 87, 90, 94, 112, 121, 123
Byass, Celia, 38-9, 64
Byass, Rupert, 38-9, 59, 60, 61, 64, 71, 76

Campbell, Major-General Jock, 93, 94, 97
Carr, Bill, 15, 112, 113, 114, 115, 117, 118, 123, 130
Carson, Alan, 112, 119, 124, 126, 127
Carson de Wiart, Lieut-General Sir Adrian, 67, 68, 93
Cavell, Nurse, 56
Cavendish, Lady Andrew, 77
Chalk, Trooper, 36
Chamberlain, Neville, 9
Cheeseman, Trooper, 36
Chorley, Corporal, 53-4
Christie, Rupert, 156
Churchill, Gerald, 90, 91-2, 123
Churchill, Sir Winston, 61, 67, 74, 77, 78, 79, 129, 130, 163
Clark-Kennedy, John, 36, 69
Clifton-Brown, Geoffrey, 78
Coningham, Air-Marshal Sir Arthur, 130
Cox, Captain, 83, 84
Cripps, Brigadier B., 12

Darraugh, Sergeant, 110
Davies, Wilfred, 51, 156
Dawnay, David, 67-8
de Kerzauzon de Penandef, Bob, 108-9, 110, 111
de la Falaise, Henry, 26-7, 28, 35, 43, 55, 63, 64
de Larminet, General, 106, 109, 110
de Piro, Michael, 86
de Pourtalès, Comte, 23
Dill, Field-Marshal Sir John, 22

Ditton, Sergeant, 28, 29, 35-6
Dowell, 'Stinker', 27, 28, 29, 87, 104

Ellen, Sergeant-Major, 127, 129
Erne, John (Earl of), 35, 47, 55, 66, 67
Errington, George, 131

Farquhar, Peter, 65
Fenwick, François, 26
Field, Harold, 70
Fisher, Major-General B., 14
Fitzgerald, Intelligence Corps, 106, 109, 111
Fitzgerald, Irish Guards, ADC, 67
Flower, Philip, 97, 98-102, 142
Fortune, Major-General Sir Victor, 153
Francis, Sergeant, 137, 139, 141
Frazer, Donald, 47, 162
Fuller, Gerry, 128

Gale, Colonel, 83, 84, 85, 89
Galley, Colonel, 98, 120
Garmoyle, Hugo (Viscount), 123
Gemmell, Arthur, 80, 90, 113
Godwin-Austen, Lieut-General A. R., 92
Gort, Field-Marshal Lord, 24, 48, 62
Gott, Lieut-General W. ('Strafer'), 92, 115
Gregson, Charles, 70, 103, 104
Gregson, Molly, 70
Griffiths, Trooper, 36, 42, 49
Grissell, Michael, 161

Hall, Basil, 36-7
Harding, Field-Marshal Lord, 104, 105
Harewood, *see* Lascelles
Harriman, Averel, 78
Harrison, David, 156, 161
Henderson, John, 106
Heydeman, Major-General Cecil, 18-19
Heyworth, Reggie, 95
Hope, 'Halfpenny', 10
Hope, Septima (Aunt Fetty), 11, 19, 147
Hopkinson, Colonel 'Hoppy', 33
Horrocks, Lieut-General Sir Brian, 134
Horsbrugh-Porter, Andrew, 21, 23, 24, 32, 37, 38, 40, 41, 43, 45, 46, 47, 50, 53, 64, 66, 71, 80, 81
Howard, Henry, 132, 133

James, Jimmy, 153, 154
Jeffreys, Christopher, 62
Joffre, Marshal, 30
Joffre, Mme, 30
Johnson, Tony, 113
Johnson, Sergeant, 49

Kennedy, Joseph, 26, 63
Kidston (later Kidston-Montgomerie), George, 127, 163
Killick, steward, 85
Koenig, General, 106-7, 115
Kopanski, General, 105

Lancaster, Colonel C.G., 79
Lascelles, George (later Lord Harewood), 162
Laurelle, Lieutenant, 106
Lawrence, 'Uncle', 16
Leese, Lieut-General Sir Oliver, 70, 134
Lewis, Sergeant, 36, 55
Lindsay, Mick, 105
Llewellen-Palmer, Tim, 13
Lumsden, Lieut-General Herbert, 20, 22, 25, 33, 34, 36, 46, 54, 59, 62, 63, 64, 69, 90, 92, 96, 102, 115, 116, 118, 119, 122, 123, 126, 134, 136, 163-4

Mabbott, Bill, 9, 16, 65, 71, 75, 96
McCreery, General Sir Richard, 14, 16, 18, 19, 71, 122, 163

Macmanaway, Revd Godfrey, 31, 65
McNulty, Mr, 12
Maguire, Bob, 126
Mann, Edward, 39, 72, 89, 114, 116, 121, 122, 126, 129, 134, 139, 142
Marriott, Major-General Sir John, 96
Marti, Capitaine, 106
Messervy, General Sir Frank, 96, 117, 120
Miller, Lieut-General Sir Euan, 154
Miller-Mundy, Peter, 39
Montgomery, Field-Marshal Lord, 18, 62, 129, 130, 134, 163
Morgan, Trooper, 36
Morris, Tim, 15, 65-6
Morrison-Bell, Charles, 84
Muir, Kim, 13
Munro-Hinds, Leslie, 138
Murray-Smith, George, 14, 91

Nares, Geoffrey, 111, 125, 126, 128, 129
Newman, Charles, 155, 164
Norrie, Lieut-General Lord, 68, 69, 78, 92, 112, 120

Orr-Lewis, Ann (Lady), 166

Palmer, Rodney, 21, 34, 71, 79, 94, 95
Peake, Roger, 137
Peel, Teddy and Nora, 131
Plant, Corporal, 139, 141-2
Poole, Jack, 157

Ransome, Captain 'Shaggy', 12, 13, 15, 33
Reid, Miles, 154-5, 157
Richardson, John, 118, 123
Ritchie, General Sir Neil, 153
Robinson, Sergeant-Major, 120, 126-7, 137
Roddick, Andrew, 36, 55
Rodriguez, Emmita, 26, 27, 63
Rommel, Field-Marshal Erwin, 93, 108, 115, 120, 140-1
Russell, Conrad, 80

Savill, Kate, 163
Scott, Lady George, 37
Scott-Cockburn, Brigadier, 93, 95, 114
Seybold, Hauptman, 159
Shears, Charles, 160
Sinclair, Christopher, 123
Smallridge, Trooper W., 31-2, 34, 41, 60, 82, 87, 90, 92, 97, 113, 132
Smith, David, 39, 62
Smith, 'Dusty', 12
Smith, Gordon ('Long Distance'), 66
Smith, Ian ('British'), 15, 21, 39, 66, 71
Sparkes, Sergeant, 36, 45
Speke, Neil, 9, 33, 73, 83, 86, 104, 105, 111, 131, 138
Stimpson, John, 69, 70, 95, 126, 138
Strang, Sam, 79
Swanson, Gloria, 26
Swayne, Ronnie, 155, 165
Swinburn, Henry, 154, 159

Tate, Captain, 87
Tennant, Pauline, 72
Tree, Sergeant-Major, 35, 36
Trent, Lady, 29, 30

Wainman, Bill, 113
Warre, Tony, 15, 18, 21, 33
Wavell, Field-Marshal Lord, 77
Wellesley, Valerian, 128-9
West, Lieut-Colonel, 102-3, 114
Weymouth, Daphne (Lady), 80
Wetherly, Toby, 125, 126
Willis, 'Dozy', 20, 24, 29, 38, 39, 41, 71, 72, 79
Windus, Bob, 161
Wormald, John, 78
Wyndham, Mark, 126, 136
Wyndham, Ursula, 163